LUCENT LIBRARY of HISTORICAL ERAS

THE INDUSTRIAL REVOLUTION IN THE UNITED STATES

LUCENT LIBRARY *of* HISTORICAL ERAS

THE INDUSTRIAL REVOLUTION IN THE UNITED STATES

DON NARDO

LUCENT BOOKS
A part of Gale, Cengage Learning

GALE
CENGAGE Learning

Detroit • New York • San Francisco • New Haven, Conn • Waterville, Maine • London

LIBRARY OF CONGRESS CATALOGING-IN-PUBLICATION DATA

Nardo, Don, 1947–
 The industrial revolution in the United States / by Don Nardo.
  p. cm. -- (The lucent library of historical eras)
 Includes bibliographical references and index.
 ISBN 978-1-4205-0153-7 (hardcover)
 1. Industrial revolution--United States--History. I. Title.
 HC105.N26 2009
 330.973'05--dc22

                                                           2008053505

Lucent Books
27500 Drake Rd.
Farmington Hills, MI 48331

ISBN-13: 978-1-4205-0153-7
ISBN-10: 1-4205-0153-4

Printed in the United States of America
 2 3 4 5 6 7 13 12 11 10

Printed by Bang Printing, Brainerd, MN, 2nd Ptg., 02/2010

Contents

Foreword

Looking back from the vantage point of the present, history can be viewed as a myriad of intertwining roads paved by human events. Some paths stand out—broad highways whose mileposts, even from a distance of centuries, are clear. The events that propelled the rise to power of Germany's Third Reich, its role in World War II, and its eventual demise, for example, are well defined and documented.

Other roads are less distinct, their route sometimes hidden from view. Modern legislatures may have developed from old tribal councils, for example, but the links between them are indistinct in places, open to discussion and interpretation.

The architecture of civilization—law, religion, art, science, and government—as well as the more everyday aspects of our culture—what we eat, what we wear—all developed along the historical roads and byways. In that progression can be traced every facet of modern life.

A broad look back along these roads reveals that many paths—though of vastly different character—seem to converge at a few critical junctions. These intersections are those great historical eras that echo over the long, steady course of human history, extending beyond the past and into the present.

These epic periods of time are the focus of Historical Eras. They shine through the mists of history like beacons, illuminated by a burst of creativity that propels events forward—so bright that we, from thousands of years away, can clearly see the chain of events leading to the present.

Each Historical Eras consists of a set of books that highlight various aspects of these major eras. For example, the Elizabethan England library features volumes on Queen Elizabeth I and her court, Elizabethan theater, the great playwrights, and everyday life in Elizabethan London.

The mini-library approach allows for the division of each era into its most significant and most interesting parts and the exploration of those parts in depth. Also, social and cultural trends as well as illustrative documents and eyewitness accounts can be prominently featured in individual volumes.

Historical Eras presents a wealth of information to young readers. The lively narrative, fully documented primary and secondary source quotations, maps, photographs, sidebars, and annotated bibliographies serve as launching points for class discussion and further research.

In studying the great historical eras, students also develop a better understanding of our own times. What we learn from the past and how we apply it in the present may shape the future and may determine whether our era will be a guiding light to those traveling future roads.

THE SECOND AMERICAN REVOLUTION

Every grade-school student knows that the thirteen British colonies in North America launched a rebellion against the mother country from 1776 to 1783. From this momentous war, called the American Revolution, a new nation emerged. Calling itself the United States, it was the world's first modern democracy. Over the course of more than a century, it steadily grew in power and influence until it was the richest and strongest country on the globe as well as a model for freedom-loving people everywhere.

However, America's astonishing success did not rest merely on the fact that it was a free democracy. Indeed, its success would have been quite impossible without a second revolution that followed on the heels of the first. It is commonly referred to as the Industrial Revolution. (Most historians call it the Second Industrial Revolution; the first began in Britain in the 1700s.)

Striking "Before and After" Snapshots

The Industrial Revolution in America marked a major shift from a largely agricultural economy to one that used machines and factories to manufacture goods on a large scale. It is difficult to date this pivotal series of events with any precision. Different historians assign it different dates. However, most experts agree that it began roughly in the late 1700s or early 1800s, not long after the country broke with Britain. And it continued though World War I and into the 1920s and 1930s.

The Industrial Revolution began with a relatively slow adoption of advanced industrial methods in the United States. The main exception was the textile industry, which was the first area of manufacturing to use machines on a large scale. Most other aspects of industrialization, including iron and steel production, the use of petroleum and electricity, and improvements in communications, became large scale only after the American Civil War (1861–1865). As one scholar puts it:

> The true age of the machine [in America] emerged . . . after 1870, when the use of electricity and the internal combustion engine mech-

anized virtually all aspects of manufacturing. Inventions also created whole new industries, such as the chemical and automobile businesses.[1]

Some of the "before and after" snapshots are striking. Before the Civil War, for example, it took an American farmer about sixty-one hours to produce 1 acre (.40ha) of wheat; by 1900, it took a little more than three hours. Similarly, the first U.S. mills designed to turn out large amounts of copper wire (for telegraph lines) opened in 1860. By 1880 they were

Revolution or Evolution?

Over the years, some scholars and students of the age of industrialization have complained that the term revolution, *when used in the phrase* Industrial Revolution, *is inappropriate. This argument, says Oberlin College scholar Gary J. Kornblith, a leading expert on the rise of American industry, revolves around "whether a historical process that spanned a hundred years [or more] can be properly called a revolution." After all, in the minds of many people, a revolution is a sudden, dramatic event of rather short duration. More often than not, such events as the French Revolution or American Revolution come to*

mind. However, Kornblith speaks for a majority of scholars when he adds:

The real test may be the extent of the transformation [of the United States] and the turbulence the process [of industrialization] entailed, not how long it took. Given the deep contrast between how most Americans lived in 1790 and in 1890, the term *revolution* seems to [me] more appropriate than the alternative *evolution*. But readers are encouraged to draw their own conclusions.

Gary J. Kornblith, ed., *The Industrial Revolution in America*. Boston: Houghton Mifflin, 1998, p. xvi.

producing 30,000 tons (26,786 metric tons) a year; and by 1910 they were producing 500,000 tons (446,429 metric tons). Overall, by 1890 America generated fully one-third of the globe's entire industrial output, surpassing even the former leader, Britain. This trend continued at full tilt into the twentieth century. Actually, in a sense the ongoing growth in American industry's size and sophistication never stopped. However, most historians prefer terms like *technological revolution* or *age of technology* to describe industrial and other technical advances after about 1940.

An Economic Empire Rises

The Industrial Revolution's transformation of the United States into the world's leading political, economic, and military power rested on three major developments. Perhaps most important was the creation of the country's modern transportation and communications systems. These included the extensive fleets of steamships and networks of railroad lines that made the shipment and distribution of vast amounts of manufactured goods possible. It also included the telegraph and the telephone, which significantly improved the coordination and efficiency of these networks.

The second major development, says Alfred D. Chandler, a leading authority on American industrialization,

was the coming of electricity in the 1880s, which provided a more flex-

ible source of power than steam for industrial machinery, a new means of urban transportation (the trolley and the subway), and brighter, cheaper, and safer illumination in factories, offices, and homes. . . . The third development was the beginning of the application of science to industrial processes and the creation of new and improved consumer and industrial products.[2]

In addition to these developments, another factor helped to propel the industrialization process forward and accelerate the growth of America into a world superpower. This is sometimes termed the *economic interdependence* of industries. Many industries gained power and influence from dealing with or borrowing from other industries. For instance, the steel industry strongly influenced the real estate business because builders of factories, office buildings, and houses used steel as a raw material. Similarly, the iron and steel industries contributed to the success of the railroads (whose locomotives and tracks were made of iron and steel) and the building of bridges.

The economic empire that America built from having so many successful industries therefore rested on the twin pillars of two mighty modern revolutions. One gave U.S. citizens a degree of freedom—personal, political, and economic—rarely seen in the world before 1776. The other provided them with the material and technological means to pre-

A lithograph shows the major developments of the Industrial Revolution, including the railroad, telegraph, and steamboat.

serve and protect that freedom as well as to promote it abroad. "These dual transformations," scholar John F. Kasson points out, "ultimately conjoined [came together] in a way that has shaped the character of much of [U.S.] history."[3] Indeed, the experts agree that, more than any other single factor, the Industrial Revolution made it possible for the United States to eventually rise to its current status as the world's main economic superpower.

Chapter One

THE ORIGINS OF AMERICAN INDUSTRY

Today, the United States is an industrial and technological giant with by far the world's largest and most robust economy. In 2008 the U.S. economy was more than twice as big as that of China, which boasts the second largest economy on the globe. In the same year the U.S. economy was more than six times bigger than that of the United Kingdom, also called Britain.

It is therefore hard for many modern Americans to imagine that only a little more than two centuries ago the United States lagged far behind its former mother country, Britain, which in those days was the world's economic and military superpower. In the late 1700s and early 1800s, Britain was rapidly industrializing. In the process it was swiftly moving away from its once mainly agricultural economy. But the infant United States still relied primarily on traditional farming methods and communities, and in the words of scholar Gary J. Kornblith, "The new republic's economy was essentially undeveloped, even backward."[4]

Yet that situation was destined to change in profound ways that people at the time could not foresee. In large part this was because America possessed phenomenally abundant natural resources that it would eventually begin to tap and develop. Also, U.S. inventors, machinists, and businessmen had recent British inventions and industrial accomplishments to draw on as models. Finally, so-called Yankee ingenuity became a potent factor as American inventors and entrepreneurs built on, and in time surpassed, those foreign models.

America Before Industrialization

It took many decades for industry to take hold in a major way in America, however.

Back in 1791, less than three years after the U.S. Constitution was written, only one of the founding fathers foresaw that the nation's future lay in industry and manufacturing. That year Alexander Hamilton, then serving as the first secretary of the treasury, issued his "Report on Manufactures" to Congress. He encouraged the building of factories for mass production of goods and rationalized it with the following appraisal of what he saw as an American spirit of inventiveness:

There is, in the genius of the people of this country, a peculiar aptitude for mechanical improvements. [It] would operate as a forcible reason for giving opportunities to the exercise of that species of talent by the propagation [growth] of manufactures. . . . The spirit of enterprise . . . must be less in a nation of mere cultivators, than in a nation of cultivators [and] artificers [inventors] and merchants.[5]

The United States was mostly a country of individual farmers following its independence from Britain in 1776.

Unfortunately for both Hamilton and the nation, Congress largely ignored his call for creating an industrial base in America. Most of the country's leaders agreed with another founder, Thomas Jefferson, who believed that the United States would remain a nation of farmers for many generations to come. At the time, this seemed to make sense. The country was mainly rural. In fact, only 5 percent of Americans lived in communities of twenty-five hundred people or more, and three out of every four families lived on small farms. According to Northeastern University scholar Laura L. Frader:

> Farmers relied on rudimentary equipment and time-honored practices. Most worked with wooden plows and depended on horses or cattle to pull them. Women spun thread on wooden spinning wheels or used long, grooved rods called distaffs. Weavers wove fabric on wooden looms small enough to fit into the room of a house. . . . Both men and women planted, cultivated, and harvested, while children and young people helped. Young people also milked cows, churned butter, gathered eggs, and fed farm animals.[6]

Meanwhile, only 10 percent of American workers, male and female alike, worked in manufacturing, here defined as making products for people outside the immediate family. Moreover, most of these workers made products by hand, either at home or in small workshops. A large proportion of them wove yarn or made clothes in their homes, for example. Interestingly, a few did part of the work themselves and paid neighbors to do the rest. One such small-time entrepreneur was a Maine woman named Martha Ballard, who made extra money selling cloth. She collected the wool and flax (the plant from which linen is made) and delivered it to a woman who spun them into yarn. Another neighbor wove the yarn into cloth; and still another dyed the cloth. While managing this process, Ballard earned more income as a sort of informal nurse-healer. On August 7, 1787, she recorded in her diary: "Called to Mrs. Howard's this morning to see her [sick] son. [Found] him [feeling] very low. . . . From thence to Joseph Foster's to [his] sick children. [Found them] very ill."[7] Other early American manufacturers were local village blacksmiths. They made horseshoes, nails, and various metal tools by hand and sold them, from either their homes or small shops located nearby.

Though highly industrious, these scattered, small-scale manufacturers were unable to make enough products to meet American demand. So a large proportion of manufactured goods were still imported from Britain well after the close of the American Revolution. Another reason that American manufacturers often found it difficult to compete with imports was that European-made goods were widely viewed as higher in quality. Using the example of cloth, tex-

Early American Views of Manufacturing

Most of the U.S. founding fathers did not foresee that America would become industrialized, and they promoted agriculture as the main basis for the country's economy. Thomas Jefferson, for example, often stated that manufacturing was unneeded and might even lead to corruption. In 1785 he said, "I consider [manufacturers] as the panders of vice and the instruments by which the liberties of a country are generally overturned."

Farming was much more noble and moral, Jefferson believed. He told George Washington in 1787 that agriculture "is our wisest pursuit, because it will in the end contribute most to real wealth, good morals and happiness." That same year he told James Madison: "I think our governments will remain virtuous for many centuries as long as they are chiefly agricultural. . . . When they get piled upon one another in large cities as in Europe, they will become corrupt as in Europe."

By 1817, however, Jefferson had seen the fruits of early industry and had begun to change his mind. He told a colleague: "I was once a doubter whether the labor of the cultivator . . . would not produce more value than that of the manufacturer. . . . But the inventions of later times, by labor-saving machines do as much now for the manufacturer as the earth for the cultivator."

Quoted in Eyler Robert Coates Sr., "Thomas Jefferson on Politics and Government: Commerce and Agriculture." http://etext.virginia.edu/jefferson/quotations/jeff1320.htm.

Thomas Jefferson initially felt that manufacturing was unnecessary, but changed his mind after seeing early industrial inventions.

tile industry historian Paul E. Rivard writes:

> Farm families filled the local needs for low-priced cloth in New England, while finer goods continued to be made by professional craftspeople in Europe. Imported goods were preferred by those who could afford them. . . . The domestic homespuns we find endearing today were [then] seen for what they were: coarse substitutes for the elegant products of European craftspeople.[8]

Britain Becomes the Model

It was not by accident that so many Americans (as well as people in many other countries) relied on British manufactured goods. At the time British workshops produced far more goods than those of any other nation. Moreover, British industry was rapidly becoming larger in scale. More and more mills and factories were being built in Britain, while industry was becoming more sophisticated as newer, more advanced laborsaving devices were introduced. These events and trends were pivotal, not only for Britain but also for other nations. This was especially true for the United States. Large-scale industry would not have developed in America, or at least would have taken much longer to develop, if Britain's Industrial Revolution had not provided a compelling model to follow.

Britain had many advantages that made it a global economic leader. In particular, the supremacy of the British navy helped protect British shipping and business interests.

The first major economic sector to be transformed by machines in Britain was agriculture. Before 1750, the vast majority of people there and in other parts of Europe lived in rural areas and sustained themselves by growing crops or raising animals. This situation changed significantly in the 1700s and early 1800s, partly because of the appearance of new inventions that began to mechanize farming. The first of these devices was the seed drill, introduced in 1701 by English gentleman farmer Jethro Tull (1674–1741). Mounted on four wooden wheels and pulled along by a horse, it drilled holes in the earth, dropped in seeds, then covered the holes with dirt. The seed drill and other machines or machine-made devices greatly increased crop yields in Britain. Also, because more food could be grown by fewer farmers, many people stopped farming and moved into the cities, which rapidly increased in size in the ensuing decades.

Large numbers of these new urban dwellers took jobs in the manufacturing sector, which was also being transformed by machines. In ages past, goods such as clothes, pottery, candles, metal tools, and weapons were made entirely by hand. But this hand-manufacturing system steadily gave way to machine manufacturing in the late 1700s and early 1800s. At the same time, the manner in which factory laborers accomplished their work changed. They became more specialized, with each worker or group of workers doing only one part of the process. This new system became known as division of labor.

The combination of new technological advances and the reorganization of production processes resulted in huge increases in production across England and other parts of Britain. In the spinning industry, for example, by 1820 steam-driven spindles were producing a hundred times as much thread as old-style hand-operated spindles had. The expansion of British textiles in general was equally dramatic. Between 1750 and 1770 British cotton exports increased tenfold; and by the 1830s cotton products made up half of Britain's exports. Similarly, the volume of iron and coal production increased enormously. By 1850 Britain produced at least half of the entire world's output of iron. Also by 1850, Britain produced more than half of the world's steel, two-thirds of its coal, and more than half of its manufactured goods.

These advances in iron, steel, and other industrial sectors occurred in large part because Britain possessed certain logistical advantages that most other nations did not. First and foremost, it almost literally ruled the seas. The huge British navy protected Britain's merchant ships and ensured that their business ventures were uninterrupted.

Also, during the eighteenth and nineteenth centuries Britain had a global empire with colonies in every inhabited continent. This gave the British ready access to vast amounts of timber, metal ores, and other raw materials. As a result of these and other advantages, by 1850 Britain was the global economic leader and profoundly influenced the affairs and economies of many other nations. "An entire world economy was thus built on, or rather around, Britain," says renowned scholar Eric J. Hobsbawm. "There was a moment in the world's history when Britain can be described . . . as its only [large-scale] workshop."[9]

America's Vast Industrial Potential

This immense and impressive display of invention and mass manufacturing in Britain was well under way before anyone in Britain's American colonies made even a modest attempt to industrialize. But the great industrial inequality between the two regions was destined to change, partly because of the American Revolution. That event did more than launch the independent United States. It also created a situation in which America could no longer rely totally on British manufactured goods. Yet creating a large manufacturing base far from the former mother country was no simple task.

Part of the problem was that America's agricultural economy was extremely entrenched. And only a few people, Alexander Hamilton prominent among them, were able to foresee that moving to an industrial economy would be beneficial to the nation. Also, it was difficult at first for Americans to acquire industrial knowledge from Britain, which jealously and tightly guarded the secrets of its technical developments. In fact, Britain's legislature, Parliament, actually

American cities like Philadelphia saw an enormous growth in population during the nineteenth century, creating a greater demand for manufactured products.

passed laws that banned the export of textile machinery and technical knowledge about them. This legislation discouraged machinists and engineers from moving to the United States or other nations and passing on their knowledge of industry to foreigners.

Nevertheless, no matter how daunting the task seemed at the time, the new nation possessed an enormous potential for successful industrialization. First, its population was increasing rapidly. And more and more of these people moved to or were born in cities, which grew rapidly. Philadelphia, America's largest city in 1776, grew from 42,000 residents in 1790 to 340,000 in 1850. In the same period, New York City's population rose from a mere 33,000 to an impressive 515,000, and it reached a staggering 1,080,000 in 1860. These growing urban populations generated a great deal of demand for manufactured products.

The United States had another untapped advantage in its vast forests, mountains, and fertile valleys, many brimming with natural resources. Among the natural resources were gigantic reserves of trees to supply wood for new construction, coal to fire the furnaces of industry, and iron and other metals to make machines, furnaces, railroad tracks, artillery guns, metal ships, and other modern equipment and devices.

Early American Experiments

Although America as a whole was at first slow to develop these potential resources on a large scale, especially industrially, some noteworthy and clever individuals did begin moving in that direction in the late 1700s and early 1800s. One was the famous American patriot Benjamin Franklin (1706–1790).

Among his many talents, he was an inventor with a particular interest in electricity, about which science knew very little at the time. The phenomenon of static electricity had been observed for many centuries. But it remained uncertain whether lightning was also a form of electricity until Franklin showed this to be the case in 1752.

By attaching a piece of metal to a kite flown during a thunderstorm, he was able to attract some lightning, which took the form of sparks identical to those in discharges of static electricity. Franklin's experiments were part of a series of

Benjamin Franklin's experiments with electricity led to practical applications of this form of energy.

Fulton Remembers His Steamboat

In a letter to an unknown friend, Robert Fulton described the somewhat shaky opening moments of the historic first voyage of his steamboat in August 1807.

The moment arrived in which the word was to be given for the boat to move. My friends were in groups on the deck. There was anxiety mixed with fear among them. They were silent, sad and weary. I read in their looks nothing but disaster, and almost repented of my efforts. The signal was given and the boat moved on a short distance and then stopped and became immovable. To the silence of the preceding moment, now succeeded murmurs of discontent, and agitations, and whispers and shrugs. I could hear distinctly repeated—"I told you it was so; it is a foolish scheme: I wish we were well out of it." . . . [But then] I went below and examined the machinery, and discovered that the cause was a slight maladjustment of some of the work. In a short time it was obviated [fixed]. The boat was again put in motion. She continued to move on. All [of the passengers] were still incredulous. None seemed willing to trust the evidence of their own senses.

Quoted in Alice Crary Sutcliffe, "Robert Fulton and the *Clermont*," Hudson River Maritime Museum. www .hrmm.org/diglib/sutcliffe/chapter4-1.html.

Robert Fulton's first steamboat voyage took place in August 1807.

discoveries about electricity that led to its practical application in factories and homes decades later.

More immediately useful for large-scale manufacturing was the cotton gin, introduced by American inventor Eli Whitney (1765–1825) in 1793. A relatively simple device, it separated cotton fiber from the plant's seeds much more efficiently than could be done by hand. As a result, a worker could produce fifty times more cotton than before. At the time, American textile mills were in their infancy, so the cotton gin at first mainly benefited Britain; its many prosperous mills imported large amounts of inexpensive cotton from America, which helped to expand the British Industrial Revolution.

The most notable early American contribution to the onrush of industrialization was the practical river steamboat. Steam engines were built and applied to industry in Britain in the 1700s by several inventors, including James Watt (1736–1819). And a Scottish engineer, William Symington (1764–1831), demonstrated the first steamboat in 1802. American inventor Robert Fulton (1765–1815) saw this boat up close and soon afterward constructed his own steamboats. Using a British-built engine, one of Fulton's ships steamed up the Hudson River from New York City to Albany in 1807. The sight of this vessel, which belched out large amounts of black smoke and sparks, struck many witnesses—who had never heard of a steamboat—with awe and fear. An eyewitness recorded:

> The crews of many sailing vessels shrunk beneath their decks at the terrific sight, while others prostrated themselves [laid on the ground] and besought Providence [God] to protect them from the approach of the horrible monster which was marching on the tide and lighting its path by the fire that it vomited.[10]

People quickly got used to steam-powered riverboats on the Hudson and other American rivers, however. By 1820, 69 of these craft operated on the Ohio and Mississippi alone; by 1830 that number had risen to 187; and by 1850 there were 536. A sign of the times, these boats signaled that the Industrial Revolution had begun to take hold in the United States. However, no one yet had an inkling of how huge it would eventually become and how completely and permanently it would reshape the nation.

Chapter Two

TEXTILE MILLS
LEAD THE WAY

The first sector of the early U.S. economy to become industrialized was textiles. Indeed, the rise of the textile industry marked the beginning of a new age of mass production and major economic expansion in America. Though overall U.S. industry still lagged far behind that of Britain, the growing success of American textiles signaled to the world that a potential manufacturing giant was starting to awaken and flex its muscles.

Colonial Textiles

Americans had certainly made many of their own clothes all through colonial times (the 1600s and early to middle 1700s). But yarn spinning, weaving, and clothes making had been strictly household-centered activities. The methods and seeds had originally come from Britain, which, be-fore it became industrialized, long had a tradition of "homespun" cloth and clothes. Also, as in Britain, home-centered textile activities in early America were mainly the domain of women workers and remained so for generations to come. In the early 1800s a Maine woman wrote:

> It is well known that [cloth making] is confined almost wholly to the female part of the families, to whom other modes of profitable employment are generally not open [and] a large part of whom, without this manufacture, would probably have the opportunity to contribute but little to the general wealth of the state.[11]

Meanwhile, those colonists who could afford it continued to import British-made clothes, which were generally

Before the Industrial Revolution, most Americans made their own clothes by hand at home.

viewed as being higher in quality than native-made ones.

The desire to buy British yarn, cloth, and clothes began to dissipate, however, as relations between the colonies and the mother country deteriorated in the 1760s and 1770s. And shortly after the American Revolution, many Americans talked about steadily replacing these imports with American-made textiles. Not long after becoming president in 1789, George Washington wrote in a letter: "I hope it will not be a great while before it will be unfashionable for a gentleman to appear in any other dress [except that made in America]. Indeed, we have already been too long subject to British prejudices."[12]

But to the disappointment of Washington and those who agreed with him, at first American-made textiles could not compete with British ones. Britain produced textiles in larger quantities and more cheaply in its sophisticated and efficient textile mills. According to textile historian Paul E. Rivard:

> After the American Revolution, merchants in the new nation discovered the extent of their disadvantage. British merchants continued to flood the American marketplace with inexpensive cotton yarn and cloth. America had won the war, but dependency on British manufacturing seemed greater than ever. The daunting power of British industry was apparent with each cargo of goods arriving at American wharves.[13]

Some American entrepreneurs saw this not only as an unacceptable dependence on foreigners but also as an opportunity waiting to be exploited. "Immediate efforts were needed," Rivard adds, "to promote manufacturing in the new nation, an effort born of both patriotism and envy."[14]

British Textile Models

Those Americans who desired to create a native textile industry in the United States recognized that they had one important initial advantage. Namely, they did not have to spend decades inventing and developing basic textile machinery and factory methods, as early British inventors and entrepreneurs had. Because British models of these devices and methods already existed, they could be imported to or imitated in America. A few farsighted Americans realized that the growing British textile industry might be imitated in America and create new jobs and economic expansion for the young nation.

Among the key inventions that had fueled the rise of Britain's increasingly successful textile industry was the so-called flying shuttle, which became widely popular in the 1760s and 1770s. It was invented by an English clockmaker named John Kay (1704–1780). Before this breakthrough, the average loom operator passed a wooden stick called a shuttle back and forth, thereby interweaving the vertical threads (the warp) and the horizontal threads (the weft). Kay's new invention featured a shuttle that glided on wheels. Small hammers struck the shuttle, driving it through the warp and allowing a weaver to make twice as much cloth in a given amount of time.

Another important new textile device was the spinning jenny, invented by Englishman James Hargreaves (1720–1778). Hargreaves got some of the ideas for it from fellow countryman Thomas Highs. One modern expert describes it as

a rectangular [wooden] frame mounted on four legs with a row of vertical spindles at one end. Two parallel wooden rails were mounted on a carriage that slid back and forth. Cotton . . . could then be passed between the two rails and wound on the spindles. A spinner could move the carriage with one hand and turn the handle for the spindles with the other. . . . The spinning jenny enabled a single worker to replace numerous spinners.[15]

Because it sped up the process and saved money, use of the device rapidly spread. By the late 1770s at least twenty thousand spinning jennies were in operation in British mills.

Meanwhile, an Englishman named Richard Arkwright (1732–1792) was developing and distributing a machine

The English invented several machines to aid in the production of cloth, including the spinning jenny shown at the center of this illustration.

called the water frame. Also based partly on ideas of Thomas Highs, with whom Arkwright was acquainted, it consisted of a wooden wheel connected to four pairs of rollers. These stretched cotton yarn, which then moved to a series of spindles that twisted and wound it. The term *water* in *water frame* referred to the fact that it was originally powered by rotating waterwheels embedded in streams and rivers. Cotton-spinning mills like Arkwright's swiftly multiplied across Britain, numbering about nine hundred by 1800.

Still another pivotal British textile invention was the spinning mule of Samuel Compton (1753–1827), introduced in 1779. It effectively combined elements of the spinning jenny and the water frame. A single spinning mule did the work of more than two hundred old-style hand-driven spinning wheels.

A few years later (in the 1780s), English clergyman and inventor Edmund Cartwright (1743–1823) introduced the power loom. It featured a cleverly designed array of levers, springs, and gears. At first these parts moved via wheels powered by horses and other animals, but soon this approach gave way to steam power. Slowly but steadily, power looms spread across Britain; by 1813, roughly twenty-four hundred were in use; by 1829, that number had increased to fifty-five thousand.

The First American Mills

Hoping to begin building their own cloth-making mills, a few enterprising Americans began copying these British textile machines in the 1780s. In 1789 a

Mill Towns Sprout Up

During the early 1800s dozens of villages and towns grew up around textile mills that had been erected along streams and rivers in America's New England states. One local resident later recalled this process of taming the former wilderness:

In the most rocky and desolate situations, avoided by all human beings since the settling of the Pilgrims as the image of loneliness and barrenness, amid rocks and stumps and blasted trees, there is a waterfall. Taking its stand here, the genius of our age calls into almost instantaneous life a bustling village. Here factories are erected in this barren waste, and suddenly a large population is gathered. For this population everything necessary to the social state is created.

Quoted in Steve Dunwell, *Run of the Mill*. Boston: David R. Godine, 1978, p. 69.

The first cotton mill in America was established by Samuel Slater in Pawtucket, Rhode Island.

Rhode Island mechanic (then defined as someone skilled with tools), Daniel Anthony, tinkered together his own versions of the spinning jenny and water frame. Not long after he moved them to some rented space in Pawtucket, Rhode Island, a local merchant, Moses Brown, bought the building. Determined to build the first U.S. spinning mill, Brown directed Anthony to collect and/or build more makeshift machines.

Brown's next move was destined to bring him success and transform the textile industry in New England. He hired English mechanic Samuel Slater (1768–1835), who immigrated to America late in 1789. (He traveled in disguise because

he was violating laws intended to keep industrial trade secrets from leaving Britain.) Closely familiar with British textile machines, Slater began building them from memory, quickly proving his worth. Brown put him in charge of operations in the new mill, which they constructed in 1790 on the Blackstone River in Pawtucket.

Slater also became Brown's business partner. They built a second mill in Pawtucket in 1793, today called the Slater Mill. This was so successful that Slater decided to break with Brown and strike out on his own. In 1798 Slater opened a third mill with his brother John, and over time he constructed more mills—a total of thirteen—which made him a millionaire. After his death, many came to call him the father of America's Industrial Revolution.

Most of these mills were located on the Blackstone River, which flows about 50 miles (80km) from Worcester, Massachusetts, to Pawtucket. (Eventually some eleven hundred textile mills were erected along the river, earning it the nickname "America's Hardest Working River.") By 1809 ninety mills had been built in New England and in New York State. Almost all were very successful. However, they and the emerging U.S. textile industry in general suffered from a serious drawback. This was a lack of versatility. Incapable of completing the entire cloth-making process, they largely spun yarn, then gave it to workers in homes and small workshops to weave. As a result, historian Kax Wilson explains,

a curious half-home, half-factory system of production ensued. For example, the cotton for Slater's mill was cleaned at home, spun at the mill, sent to other homes to be woven, then was taken back to the mill for bleaching and dyeing. It was an inefficient system that took two to three years to turn fiber into finished cloth.[16]

The Waltham System

In stark contrast, in 1809 many British textile mills were completing the whole cloth-making process, including weaving, in a single day. Moreover, more than two thousand of the machines that accomplished this weaving were power looms run by steam, while not a single power loom yet existed in America. "In New England," Rivard points out,

hand-weaving was still the only way to turn machine-spun yarns into cloth. Greater efficiency and productivity could be achieved if home weavers were replaced by factory machines. But this investor's dream posed [daunting] technological and organizational challenges.[17]

Meeting these challenges head-on was Boston merchant Francis Cabot Lowell (1775–1817), who was determined to modernize the American textile industry. To that end, in 1810, when he was thirty-six, he traveled to Britain and inspected several of its thriving mills. He was not allowed to take notes or make sketches, but he carefully memorized the designs of the power looms he saw in action. Upon his return to the United States, he and mechanic Paul Moody pieced together their own versions of these machines.

Next, Lowell joined with partners Patrick T. Jackson and Nathan Appleton to form the Boston Manufacturing Company. To raise the capital (investment money) they needed, they sold shares of the company to relatives, friends, and friends of friends at one thousand dollars a share. Then they built their first mill on the Charles River in

The Problem of Outmoded Equipment

One serious drawback of the textile mills that grew up in Rhode Island's Blackstone Valley was their tendency to become outdated rather quickly, since new, more efficient power looms and other machines frequently came on the market. A representative of one local textile company complained in 1844: "The whole of the cotton factories throughout this district, from Blackstone to Pawtucket, are of an inferior grade. Much of the machinery is old and dirty, while the work is deficient in both quantity and quality." That same year another industry insider complained: "Our establishment is very small . . . and our buildings and machinery are not after the modern improvements [i.e., not up to date], but we cannot afford to throw them by [get rid of them]."

Quoted in Steve Dunwell, *Run of the Mill.* Boston: David R. Godine, 1978, p. 77; and George S. White, *Memoir of Samuel Slater.* Philadelphia: Carpenter Street, 1836, p. 131.

Waltham (situated about 10 miles [16km] northwest of Boston). It was, in the words of one scholar, "the first integrated cotton factory in America, a factory in which all the processes—from unpacking cotton bales to packing finished cloth—were managed under one roof."[18] Once the new power looms went into action, Appleton toured the mill and found himself awestruck by their speed and efficiency. He later wrote:

> I well recollect the state of admiration and satisfaction with which we sat by the hour watching the beautiful movement of this new and wonderful machine, destined, as it evidently was, to change the character of all textile industry. . . . From the starting of the first power loom, there was no hesitation or doubt about the [impending] success of this manufacture.[19]

This new approach to cloth making in America, which appropriately became known as the Waltham system, was indeed tremendously successful. Lowell and his partners became wealthy. After Lowell died in 1817, Jackson and Appleton decided to further expand the business, which grew into what many people saw as an authentic textile empire. In 1822 they set up operations on the Merrimack River (about 30 miles [48km] north of Boston) in a village of two hundred residents. Four years later its population was twenty-five hundred, and the town was renamed Lowell in honor of the man who had brought the power loom to America. A mere eight years later (1834), Lowell had nineteen mills containing some three thousand power looms and eighty-four thousand spindles, which together turned out 27 million yards of cotton cloth annually.

In the early decades of their operation, the Lowell mills and others like them in the American Northeast principally hired young women. This was partly because spinning and weaving had long been viewed as "women's work"; also, as a matter of custom women still made far less money than men in the workplace, which allowed the owners to reap more profits. These owners set up boarding houses near the mills. The women, recruited from farms in the general region, lived in these houses under strict supervision, including mandatory church attendance. They also worked very long hours. One of these young women described her daily routine in a letter to a friend:

We go in [to the mill] at five o'clock [A.M.]. At seven we come out to breakfast. At half past seven we return to our work and stay until half past twelve [when we go to lunch]. At one . . . we return to our work and stay until seven at night. Then the evening is all our own.[20]

Still Behind the British

The rise of the American textile industry from the 1790s to the 1840s marked the beginnings of large-scale industrialization in the United States. It gave the country a factory system and a textile-manufacturing base, the output of which far exceeded that of the home-centered system of the past. In 1776 U.S. spinners and weavers had produced only a few thousand yards of

Francis Cabot Lowell and his partners Patrick T. Jackson and Nathan Appleton created a new approach to cloth making by building the first integrated cotton mill. This approach became known as the Waltham system.

Enduring the Noises in a Cotton Mill

Most of the employees in Lowell's Massachusetts mills were young women. In this excerpt from an 1844 letter, one of the mill girls, named Susan, describes the incessant loud noises she encountered when she first arrived at the mill.

When I went out at night the sound of the mill was in my ears, as of crickets, frogs, and [other woodland creatures], all mingled together in strange discord. After that it seemed as though cotton-wool was in my ears, but now I do not mind it at all. You know that people learn to sleep with the thunder of Niagara [Falls] in their ears and a cotton mill is no worse, though you wonder that we do not have to hold our breath in such a noise.

Quoted in Betina Eisler, *The Lowell Offering: Writings by New England Mill Women.* New York: Harper, 1977, p. 53.

cotton cloth each year; by 1805 the country's mills turned out 46,000 yards (42062.4m); and by 1830 they produced 142 million yards (155,293,080m).

Although this increase in efficiency and output was enormous and impressive, the U.S. textile industry was still unable to match its British counterpart. In 1846 American spindles, then numbering 2.5 million, accounted for about 9 percent of the world's total; that same year Britain had fully 60 percent of that total. Some American businessmen worried that they would never catch up to the British. But this anxiety proved needless. Americans were already beginning to develop the vast stores of energy that lay beneath their feet in the form of oil and coal; soon these would fuel the rise of the U.S. industrial complex that would come to dwarf that of Britain.

Chapter Three

NEW ENERGY SOURCES FOR POWER

For thousands of years before the advent of the Industrial Revolution, people relied on a small number of traditional energy sources to accomplish work. The oldest, of course, was simple human muscle power. Eventually humans learned to harness animals to carry supplies and people, pull wagons, turn millstones, and so forth. They also learned to burn wood to create warmth, cook food, and smelt copper and other metals. In addition, they discovered that moving water could also make millstones turn. These long remained humanity's principal energy sources. Although coal, petroleum (oil), and steam were all known and used in ancient times, their potential as sources of energy was never understood or developed in that era.

In the 1700s and early 1800s, when Britain and the United States began to industrialize, waterpower and the burn-

ing of wood were still the primary energy sources employed. For example, the first textile mills in Britain and America were all built on riverbanks to take advantage of the power of moving water. And wood remained the chief fuel for furnaces and early steam engines.

However, over time British and American innovators developed other energy sources and used them in factories as well as in private homes.

Coming to Depend on the "Black Rock"

Although coal was mined and burned in small quantities in colonial America, most people burned wood to warm their homes and shops and to power forges and furnaces. This seemed to make sense at the time; the colonists had access to immense forests with what appeared to be limitless stands of trees. As these forests began to disappear, however, some Americans realized that wood was actually a limited resource that should be conserved. Partly for this reason, they came to view coal as an alternative source of energy.

Large-scale coal mining began in Pennsylvania and some neighboring states in the 1820s. In particular, large amounts of a particularly useful form of coal, called anthracite, were discovered in sections of western Pennsylvania. Anthracite releases unusually high levels of heat and energy when burned. The town of Pittsburgh, which had only about four hundred residents in 1790, happened to lie near these coal deposits. As a result, in only three decades it grew into a major industrial center. By 1820 its population had grown to six thousand; by 1840 it was twenty-one thousand; and by 1850 it reached forty-seven thousand.

By 1845 more than 2 million tons (200,000,000kg) coal had been mined near Pittsburgh and in other parts of western Pennsylvania. Some of the coal was used in Pittsburgh itself, where a thousand factories had been built by 1845. In particular, coal powered the furnaces of iron foundries. So many of these were erected in Pittsburgh that it became the center of iron, and later steel, production in the country.

In the years that followed, coal extraction and use continued to expand. By

Coal mining became a major industry in the United States in the nineteenth century.

The Coming of the Steam Loom

Among the more revolutionary uses for steam engines in early industry was the steam-powered loom, which appeared in the early 1820s. In his 1823 book Compendius History of Cotton Manufacture, *English economist Richard Guest describes how this device transformed the textile industry:*

The steam engine is now applied to the working of the loom, as well as to the preparatory processes [such as cleaning the fibers and spinning them into thread]. A very good hand weaver [will] weave two pieces of [cloth] per week each twenty-four yards [22m] long. A steam loom weaver . . . will in the same [amount of] time weave seven similar pieces. A steam loom factory containing two hundred looms, with the assistance of one hundred persons . . . will weave seven hundred pieces per week, of the length and quality before described. . . . It may safely be said that the work done in a steam factory containing two hundred looms would, if done by hand weavers, find employment and support for a population of more than two thousand persons.

Quoted in Brian Tierney and Joan Scott, eds., *Western Societies: A Documentary History,* vol. 2. New York: Knopf, 1984, pp. 140–43.

1860 the United States was mining 14 million tons (12.7 million metric tons) of coal each year; 39 million tons (35.4 million metric tons) were mined in 1870; 100 million tons (91 million metric tons) in 1884; and an astounding 350 million tons (316 million metric tons) in 1900. Throughout most of the nineteenth century, factories, steamship companies, railroads, and private homes all turned to using coal for fuel and warmth. Moreover, as the iron industry steadily transformed into the steel industry in the middle to late 1800s, steel producers used enormous amounts of coal to fuel their furnaces. By the end of the century, coal provided almost three-quarters of the country's energy.

An additional by-product of the coal industry's success was its support and promotion of other major industries. Iron and steel production are perhaps the most obvious examples. But the effect that increased coal production (especially in Pennsylvania and other eastern states) had on the emerging railroads was also enormous. According to scholar Barbara Freese:

Apart from a couple of relatively minor exceptions, the anthracite mine operators were the first Americans to use rails, and they greatly advanced the science of building railways. . . . Five railway [companies] so intermingled with the anthracite trade that coal and railroading were often considered a single industry.[21]

Steam: A Symbol of Early Industry

Coal was not only carried by early trains, it also powered the steam locomotives that pulled them. Like coal, steam power encouraged the growth of a wide range of industries. In fact, the steam engine was one of the key inventions of the Industrial Revolution, and many experts view it as the main symbol of the industrial age. No single person can be credited with this device, as a number of British and American inventors had a hand in its development over time. Steamships, steam-powered locomotives, and steam-driven looms all developed from or built upon the work of previous inventors and machinists.

The first significant example of that work was the use of steam engines to pump water out of coal mines. In 1698 English inventor Thomas Savery (1650–1715) created a primitive steam-driven pump. Somewhat more complex and considerably more efficient was a version introduced by another Englishman, Thomas Newcomen, in 1712. It had a single cylinder and piston arrangement, somewhat similar to, but larger than, those in modern car engines. Steam from a simple boiler heated the cylinder, making the piston move upward; then the cylinder cooled as the steam condensed, and air pressure caused the piston to move downward. These upward and downward motions in turn made rods attached to the pump move, thereby powering the pump.

As the years went by, other inventors tried to improve Newcomen's engine. The most successful of them was Scottish inventor James Watt (1736–1819). In 1760 he introduced a seemingly simple design

One of the premier inventions of the Industrial Revolution was the steam engine. Pictured here is a diagram of Thomas Newcomen's steam engine, which he introduced in 1712.

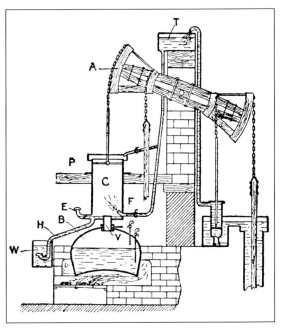

change that markedly increased the engine's efficiency. Watt devised a way to make the steam generated in the engine go into a separate chamber, in which it condensed and cooled. In this way, the steam cylinder did not constantly cool down and reheat but rather stayed hot; that used considerably less fuel.

Watt's steam engines were not only efficient but also versatile enough to do more than merely pump water out of mines. By 1824 they were used in nearly every British industry and manufacturing process. They hoisted coal up mine shafts, ran machines that hauled and threshed grain, powered forges and other machines in iron foundries, made train locomotives and large ships move, and powered all manner of textile machines, including large-scale looms. By 1835, 75 percent of Britain's cotton-making textile machines operated by steam power.

Steamboats and Locomotives

In the United States, meanwhile, Robert Fulton's pioneering work in applying steam power to ships, accomplished between 1807 and 1815, was paying off in a big way. By the 1830s steamboats carried a significant proportion of U.S. raw materials and trade goods through the nation's rivers and coastal regions. Even before Fulton's success, other American inventors had experimented with steam power. Clockmaker John Fitch (1743–1798), for instance, had tinkered together a primitive steamboat in 1787. He had also attempted to apply steam to an early version of the railroad locomotive. But Fitch's engines never saw practical use, mainly because most Americans were not yet ready for such innovations. As one modern observer puts it:

The United States of the 1790s remained primarily an agricultural society unappreciative of machinery and invention. Fitch was a man who lived ahead of his time, and his pioneering locomotive, as well as his pioneering steamboat, led to no further development of the invention. Soon both had been forgotten.[22]

In late-eighteenth-century Britain, however, such innovations were appreciated. In the late 1700s English inventor Richard Trevithick (1771–1833) in a sense picked up where Fitch had left off. Trevithick built an engine in which the steam was under much higher pressure than in Fitch's engine, or even in Watt's engines. Trevithick's version could accomplish more work, therefore. He mounted the device on wheels, creating the first practical locomotive.

Other inventors built on these early developments. They turned out improved versions of Watt's, Fitch's, Fulton's, and Trevithick's engines. And by the mid-1800s steam engines powered key machines in nearly every industry in Britain and the United States.

An Explosion of Oil Drilling

Coal and steam (largely fueled by coal) were the leading energy sources of the

Newcomen's Steam Engine

A modern expert on boilers and other industrial equipment offers this simplified description of the workings of the steam pump built by Englishman Thomas Newcomen.

Newcomen's engine consisted of a boiler in which the steam was generated. [The boiler rested beside a large upright beam.] One side of the beam was attached by a chain to the pump at the base of the mine, and the chain at the other side suspended a piston within a cylinder [located above the boiler]. The cylinder was open at the top end [to] the atmosphere. . . . [First] steam was admitted into the cylinder. [Then] cold water [entered] the cylinder, thus condensing the steam and reducing the pressure under the piston. The atmospheric pressure above then pushed the piston down in the power stroke. This raised the working parts of the pump, but their weight immediately returned the beam to its original position [and] the process started all over again.

Quoted in Eastex Instruments, "Newcomen Steam Engine." www.eastexinstruments.com/newcomen_steam_engine.htm.

Industrial Revolution in the 1850s. But they soon faced serious competition from a new and versatile fuel source—petroleum. Oil began to be extracted from the ground and used in both factories and homes in the 1850s. In 1853 a bright, ambitious New York attorney, George Bissell (1821–1884), observed a primitive oil-drilling operation in Pennsylvania. The drill brought a small amount of oil up to the surface; workers soaked it up with blankets, then drained the blankets over barrels.

In those days petroleum was used mainly for medicinal purposes. It struck Bissell that the oil could also be used as a lubricant for industrial machines and converted into kerosene to fuel lamps. Scholar Daniel Yergin points out:

The techniques required for refining petroleum into kerosene had already been commercialized with coal-oils. And an inexpensive lamp had been developed that could satisfactorily burn kerosene. In essence, what Bissell [was] trying to do was discover a new source for the raw material that went into an existing, established process.[23]

Seeing the moneymaking potential of petroleum, Bissell found some investors and formed the Pennsylvania Rock Oil

John D. Rockefeller and his company, Standard Oil, gained a monopoly over the new oil industry.

Company. They developed drilling techniques similar to those long used in boring for salt. In August 1859 their oil derrick, the world's first, began pumping oil, and by year's end they had extracted 2,000 barrels. Soon many other entrepreneurs set up their own oil rigs, leading to a veritable explosion of oil drilling and refining. In 1860 U.S. oil rigs drilled 500,000 barrels; by 1862 that number had increased to 3 million barrels; and by 1870 kerosene refined from oil had become the principal fuel for lamps in America. By this time, moreover, some companies had begun to refine oil into gasoline, at first used as an industrial solvent and cleaning fluid.

The year 1870 turned out to be an important one for U.S. industry for another reason. Businessman John D. Rockefeller (1839–1937) and his partners established the Standard Oil Company. Rockefeller bought up most of the existing oil refineries, thereby cornering the petroleum

Busting Standard Oil's Trust

Industrialist John D. Rockefeller founded the Standard Oil Company in 1870. Nine years later he went a step further by establishing the Standard Oil Trust, a central committee of oil executives who operated what was essentially a monopoly of the oil-refining industry.

The trust's subsequent ruthless business practices drove almost all of Rockefeller's competitors out of business. After numerous complaints about the situation, in 1904 President Theodore Roosevelt launched an investigation. As a result of its findings, in November 1906 the federal government filed suit against Standard Oil. The company was accused of violating the Sherman Antitrust Act of 1890 by fixing prices, abusing its monopoly, and other shady practices. In 1911 the U.S. Supreme Court ruled against Standard Oil, ordering it to break itself up into several smaller, independent companies within six months. Among these companies were those that later became the oil and gas giants Exxon, Sohio, Mobil, Chevron, Amoco, and Conoco.

John D. Rockefeller founded the Standard Oil Company and the Standard Oil Trust, which created a monopoly in the oil industry.

market. By 1877, when he was just thirty-eight, he controlled 90 percent of all the oil refined in the United States.

Not long afterward, the petroleum industry expanded still further. Some 26 million barrels were pumped in 1880. And large oil deposits were discovered in Ohio in the 1880s, in California in 1892, and in Texas and Oklahoma in the 1890s and early 1900s. Significantly, these finds coincided with the emergence of a huge new market for oil—gasoline for early automobiles. Adding the automobile industry to existing uses for petroleum brought the yearly amount of oil drilled in America to more than 440 million barrels by 1920.

Applying Electricity to Industry

Even as petroleum was rising to prominence in the late nineteenth century, another potent energy source—electricity—was undergoing intensive development. In his experiments in the 1700s, Benjamin Franklin had made an important stride by theorizing about the positive and negative properties of an electric current. In 1831 another American scientist, Joseph Henry (1797–1878), went a step further. He built a coil magnet (an iron magnet wrapped with a coil of wire) that produced an electric field.

Only a few months later, English chemist Michael Faraday (1791–1867) constructed a more complex arrangement of coil magnets. Later he built an electric generator. Henry heard about this breakthrough and built his own version, which used an electric current to move a wheel. These devices became the basis for simple but effective electric motors that could be used to power machines.

More advances in electric power came from the experiments of the prolific American inventor Thomas A. Edison (1847–1931). In 1879 he and his associates perfected the electric lightbulb. They also devised a method for distributing electric lighting throughout a city. Another important pioneer of electricity was Serbian-born American inventor Nikola Tesla (1856–1943). In the late 1800s he made huge strides in developing the principles of alternating current (AC), which came to be used in factories and homes across the United States. The new technology developed by these and other inventors spread rapidly, and by 1920 electricity had replaced petroleum products like kerosene as energy sources for lighting.

The work of Henry, Faraday, Edison, and other innovators had a profound effect on ongoing industrialization. Electrical energy could be sent from a single central generating source to many distant places. Also, it could be used to power engines and motors of any size. In addition, the various applications of electricity spawned a huge new industry, including not only generating stations but also the manufacturing of electrical equipment and appliances of numerous kinds. Finally, people found that electricity was a versatile source of light and heat.

English chemist Michael Faraday built an electric generator which, along with American scientist Joseph Henry's version, became the basis for electric motors used to power machines.

Thus, factories in the United States, Britain, and other industrialized nations installed electric lighting. And by the late 1800s electric motors had begun to replace steam engines in the vast majority of factories in these countries. In these ways, as had happened earlier with coal, steam, and petroleum, electricity both sped up the Industrial Revolution and made industry more flexible.

Chapter Four

TRANSPORTATION AND COMMUNICATIONS

When someone utters the words *industrial revolution,* certain iconic images (key symbols) immediately come to mind. Among them are a hissing steam engine, a bustling factory assembly line, white-hot molten iron in a blast furnace, and black smoke pouring from tall smokestacks. Much less clichéd and dramatic are the images of a road stretching to the horizon, some metal railroad tracks winding through a meadow, and a row of wooden poles with a wire attached. Yet these last three images exhibit products of industrialization just as important and far-reaching in their effects as the first four.

Indeed, in addition to allowing people to manufacture more goods faster and cheaper, the Industrial Revolution provided people with the means to carry those goods farther, faster, and more economically. The steamboat and train (pulled by the steam locomotive) hugely expanded trade. That boosted the economic growth of Britain, the United States, and other industrialized nations. These new, advanced modes of transportation, and eventually the automobile, also allowed *people* to travel farther, faster, and more often. The networks of train tracks and roads that relentlessly spread across the United States thereby became symbols of the nation's prosperity and the increased mobility of its citizens.

Because both goods and people traveled longer distances than ever before, staying in touch with them became more difficult. Messages sometimes took several days or even several weeks to cross oceans, vast plains, and towering mountain ranges. Faster means of communication were sorely needed, and industry's ever-busy inventors and entrepreneurs provided the necessary technology. The telegraph—and not long afterward the telephone—reduced communication times to mere seconds, allowed information to flow faster, and made business more efficient.

One reason for examining transportation and communications together is that they were (and still are) closely related. This was especially true of the railroad and telegraph, which usually followed the same routes, worked in tandem, and altered America in similar ways. As one noted scholar points out, for example, these two major new products of industry swiftly made a gigantic continent look much smaller. Before their coming, he says,

the trip from New York [to Chicago] took well over two weeks. Shortly thereafter, it took less than two days. Even more striking was the accelerated flow of *information* after the arrival of the telegraph. . . . Messages that had once taken weeks to travel

The establishment of the telegraph system revolutionized communication in the nineteenth century by allowing people to send messages across the country in minutes rather than the weeks it took with the Pony Express.

between Chicago and the east coast now took minutes and seconds. Railroad and telegraph systems...shrank the whole perceptual universe of North America. Because people experience distance more in hours than in miles, New York, Chicago, and the Great West quite literally grew closer as the lines of wire and rail proliferated among them.[24]

Roads, Canals, and Steamships

Well before the advent of trains, the telegraph, and even practical steam engines, Americans traveled and carried goods from place to place. At first, the only means of transportation through inland regions were walking, pack animals, wagons, barges, and sailing ships (where there were rivers to convey them). These were either slow or expensive or both. During and after the American Revolution, the need for new roads to connect towns and cities and for canals to link rivers to cities became increasingly evident. One of the nation's founding fathers, James Madison, called for building "a comprehensive system of roads and canals."[25]

However, nothing close to a comprehensive system was attempted at first, mostly because building long roads and canals was very costly. Of the few major paved public roads constructed in the country's early decades, the first was the Philadelphia and Lancaster Turnpike. Completed in 1795 by engineer John L.

MacAdam, it ran 62 miles (100km) from Lancaster, Pennsylvania, to Philadelphia.

Much more ambitious was the so-called National Road, built between 1811 and 1818. It stretched a distance of 620 miles (1,000km) from Cumberland, Maryland, to Wheeling, Virginia (now in West Virginia). Linking the Potomac and Ohio rivers, the road provided a convenient means for early settlers to travel westward through the Appalachian Mountains into the Ohio Valley. Over time, secondary roads branched off from

The Erie Canal was one of the most impressive engineering feats of the early nineteenth century.

these trunk arteries. However, several more decades would pass before complex modern road systems began to take shape in America (thanks largely to the coming of automobiles).

Canal building also proceeded slowly across the early American landscape. By 1812, when war broke out again between Britain and the United States, only three canals had been completed. The Santee Canal in South Carolina ran for 22 miles (35km), as did the Dismal Swamp Canal in Virginia, while the Middlesex Canal in Massachusetts was 27 miles (44km) long. These increased the volume of trade and ease of travel in their local regions. But both their lengths and impacts were dwarfed by the Erie Canal,

The Erie Canal's Enormous Impact

New York State's official Web site about the canals the state built during the Industrial Revolution provides this well-worded description of the impact of the Erie Canal after its completion in 1825.

The effect of the Canal was immediate and dramatic and settlers poured west. The explosion of trade prophesied by [New York's] Governor [Dewitt] Clinton began, spurred by freight rates from Buffalo to New York of $10 per ton by Canal, compared with $100 per ton by road. In 1829, there were 3,640 bushels of wheat transported down the Canal from Buffalo. By 1837 this figure had increased to 500,000 bushels; four years later it reached one million. In nine years, Canal tolls more than recouped the entire cost of construction. Within 15 years of the Canal's opening, New York was the busiest port in America, moving tonnages greater than Boston, Baltimore and New Orleans combined. The impact on the rest of the State can be seen by looking at a modern map. With the exception of Binghamton and Elmira, every major city in New York falls along the trade route established by the Erie Canal, from New York City to Albany, through Schenectady, Utica and Syracuse, to Rochester and Buffalo. Nearly 80% of upstate New York's population lives within 25 miles [40km] of the Erie Canal.

New York State Canal Corporation, "The Erie Canal: A Brief History." www.nyscanals.gov/cculture/history/index .html.

built between 1817 and 1825. Financed by New York State, it ran 363 miles (584km) from the Hudson River to Lake Erie; it linked New York and its port with locations hundreds of miles inland. This immense and complex engineering project was not only a potent symbol and product of America's rising industrial capacity but also another major conduit for settlers moving westward from the eastern seaboard.

Between 1816 and 1840, about 3,300 miles (5,310km) of canals were built in the United States. This mileage was low considering the country's vast size and growing transportation needs. Part of the problem was the costs involved. In 1830 it required about $37,600 (equivalent to several million dollars today) to create each mile of canal.

A great deal more of the money Americans spent on transportation in the early 1800s went into the swiftly rising steamship industry. By 1850 large portions of New England and the Northeast had daily or weekly steamship runs carrying cargo or passengers. And two years later seventeen steamship companies scheduled trips from New York City to southern ports, including New Orleans, Charleston, Savannah, Jacksonville, Norfolk, Richmond, and Petersburg.

The Rise of the Railroads

However, the great fleets of steamships that had so quickly cornered the business of traders and travelers alike just as speedily declined and faded from the American scene. Most of the steam-powered ships eventually found themselves unable to compete with a new and extremely formidable mode of transportation and shipping—the railroads.

The railroad companies used their political connections and employed ruthless business practices to take customers and revenue from the steamship companies. One after another, coastal steamships stopped operating and sat useless in dockyards. Thus, as one modern expert puts it, "the railroads eventually put steamships out of business, as trains could travel faster and could operate year round."[26]

Unlike most steamboats, trains ran from the coasts far inland. Thus, as Manhattan College scholar Jeff Horn points out, for many rural Americans, who rarely saw a steamboat or a textile mill, "the railroad was often the first tangible sign of the Industrial Revolution."[27] Not only did trains carry the raw materials and finished goods of industry, but their steam locomotives and iron tracks were themselves major products of industrial processes. Also, their ability to move cargo faster and less expensively than wagons or steamships benefited businesses of all types and thereby expanded the U.S. economy. As scholar James A. Ward says:

> Lumber, coal, glass, iron construction, and lubrication businesses located anywhere near the new [railroad] lines prospered in their wake. Bankers, brokers, printers, newspaper editors, whalers, even sandwich-makers cashed in on the new riches. Railways equally benefited shippers, importers and exporters, manufacturers, miners, farmers, and almost every other occupational group imaginable.[28]

This huge economic upsurge did not occur all at once. At first, the United States lagged behind Britain in both railroad technology and miles of track laid. This situation rapidly changed, however. The first working rail line in the United States was the Baltimore and Ohio Railroad, begun in 1828. It was intended to link the U.S. eastern coast with the Ohio Valley.

In the decades that followed, many more railroad companies formed and began laying track. By 1840 more than 3,000 miles (4,830km) of track existed in the country; by 1850, 9,000 miles (14,490km) had been laid; and by 1865 the United States had 35,000 miles (56,350km) of track. This was equal to the railroad mileage of all other nations combined (as well as 3.5 times that of

The Baltimore and Ohio Railroad (B&O) was the first working rail line in the United States.

Britain). The enormous increases in the size and impact of the Industrial Revolution in America after 1865 are reflected in the continuing expansion of the country's railway system. By 1900, 193,000 miles (310,700km) of track had been laid; and by 1920 it totaled a phenomenal 254,000 miles (408,800km).

In addition to their huge industrial and economic impact, the rise of the railroads profoundly affected Americans on social and personal levels. In particular, scholar William Cronon points out, they altered people's perceptions of the flow of time and the regularity of daily and weekly schedules:

Whereas earlier western stage[coach] and steamship operators had measured their service by how many trips they made in the course of a *week*, railroads measured the same service in terms of the scheduled trips they made in a *day*. On this scale, a train delayed by several hours was very late indeed, a fact that suggests how railroads changed people's ability to schedule and predict their use of time.[29]

Spanning the Continent

Perhaps nowhere else was the impact of the railroad industry on America more dramatic than in the creation of the transcontinental railroad—a railway line running from the continent's eastern coast to its western one. In the early 1800s, few Americans thought such a gigantic engineering project was needed, or even feasible. But as time went on, more and more settlers poured into the Midwest and West. Hundreds of new towns were established. And the enormous potential wealth of the land and natural resources of the West became increasingly plain. All these realities were further magnified by what came to be called Manifest Destiny; this was the idea that fate had decreed that the United States should control and exploit all the lands lying between the Atlantic and Pacific oceans.

In the 1850s, congressmen, newspaper editors, and other vocal advocates of this supposed destiny began calling for the construction of a rail line connecting the East to the West. Surveying teams scouted for the best route. And government officials finally decided on one that would run from Omaha, Nebraska, to Sacramento, California. Along the way it would traverse both the Great Plains and the forbidding barrier of the Sierra Nevada. The plan was for two companies to work inland from opposite ends of the country to accomplish the task. As historian Deborah Cadbury tells it:

> The Central Pacific Railroad Company, [based] in Sacramento . . . would start working its way east across the Sierras. At the same time [the] Union Pacific Railroad Company was authorized to move westwards from the

A Model for Ambitious Entrepreneurs

In addition to their role in transportation, American railroads provided a model for enterprising businesspeople to form large, successful companies, which became the backbone of America's economy. Historian Gary J. Kornblith explains:

Confronted with an unprecedented need for close coordination of complex operations over large geographical areas, railroad corporations introduced layers of middle managers. . . . To finance this organizational transformation and the huge cost of basic equipment and labor, the corporations sold stocks [in] amounts unprecedented for private enterprises. As a result, the New York Stock Exchange flourished. . . . These developments in turn led to the creation of a truly national market and a number of truly national companies [as] entrepreneurs in other industries adopted the railroads' business strategies. . . . For the first time, big business became a central institution in American life.

Gary J. Kornblith, ed., *The Industrial Revolution in America.* Boston: Houghton Mifflin, 1998, pp. xxi–xxii.

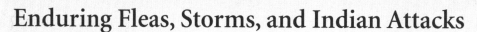

Enduring Fleas, Storms, and Indian Attacks

Historian Deborah Cadbury gives this vivid overview of living conditions among the Union Pacific's laborers as they constructed the transcontinental railroad.

As the labor force reached 10,000, the company needed a small army of cooks, supply men, and guards to keep up with the workers as they made their way across the plains. The main food supply was the 500 cattle that trotted alongside them, and most of the men were content with a diet of beef, bread, coffee, and spirits [liquor] when available. For sleeping, long 50-foot [15m] trucks were rigged with bunks, but many of the men preferred to bed down in the open to avoid the fleas and vermin that were constant companions in the cramped conditions of the trucks. Those sleeping in the open faced the legendary . . . storms that came thundering across the plains with breathtaking fury, white lightning, and beating rain. But another horror, far more terrifying than the storms, preyed on the minds of these men [namely, attacks by Indians]. Every worker slept with his gun beside him.

Deborah Cadbury, *Dreams of Iron and Steel: Seven Wonders of the Nineteenth Century.* New York: Fourth Estate, 2004, p. 171.

Missouri River, on the border between Iowa and Nebraska, where the existing railroad network ended. Somewhere in the unmapped wilderness in between, the two companies would meet.[30]

The Central Pacific broke ground on January 8, 1863. Because of delays caused by the ongoing Civil War, the Union Pacific did not start laying track until 1865. Progress, however, was swift. By March 1869 the two lines were only about 50 miles (80km) apart. On May 10 they joined tracks at Promontory Point, Utah, driving in a ceremonial golden spike to seal the deal. The news sped across the nation, and President Ulysses S. Grant received the message: "The last rail is laid! The last spike is driven! The pacific railroad is completed!"[31]

It was a pivotal moment in the country's history. The iron and other products of an industrial expansion begun in the East had penetrated the West, thereby making the union of the two regions inevitable. "The centuries-old worn buffalo trails began to disappear," Cadbury writes,

as the country shifted gear to embrace the iron and steel of the future. And as the great unstoppable iron road took the long journey east from Sacramento . . . it created one country more surely, more simply, and quickly than treaties, proclamations, and wars ever did.[32]

Advances in Communications

The reason that the news of the historic meeting in Utah spread so quickly was that separate crews had built telegraph lines alongside the railroad tracks all along the route. Thus, the Industrial Revolution was also making the nation smaller by making communications faster than ever before. Two different teams working independently, one British, the other American, had introduced workable commercial versions of the telegraph in 1837. The British team consisted of William Cooke (1806–1901) and Charles Wheatstone (1802–1875). The Americans were Samuel F.B. Morse (1791–1872) and Alfred L. Vail (1807–1859). Both devices worked by sending an electrical current through a wire. Messages could be sent by transmitting pulses of varying lengths, each pulse or combination of pulses standing for a letter of the alphabet.

The subsequent application of the new invention, including the creation of a vast network of telegraph lines, was rapid. By the mid-1860s, the Western Union Telegraph Company (established in 1851) had twenty-two thousand telegraph offices and 827,000 miles (1.3 million km) of lines spanning the East and Midwest. Moreover, in 1866 America was linked to Europe by the first transatlantic telegraph cable.

Another invention of the onrushing industrial age—the telephone—proved to be even more successful in improving human communications and making business more efficient. American inventor Alexander Graham Bell (1847–1922) patented the telephone in 1876. Between 1877 and 1893 the number of

Alexander Graham Bell's invention of the telephone improved communications and made businesses more efficient.

phones leased to customers by Bell's company increased from 3,000 to 260,000. And by 1920, the country had more than 13 million phones. Many of these phones were installed in offices, factories, warehouses, railroad stations, and other businesses. The telephone gave industry and business an easy, fast way of coordinating operations, thereby helping to expand the U.S. economy. As one expert points out, Bell's creation was

> no ordinary invention, not just another desirable consumer product.

. . . Its importance to industrial life [was] not just that it [was] another machine of production, like the spinning jenny. . . . Its importance [was] as a contribution to the organized bureaucracy that is the hallmark of modern industrial society.[33]

In these ways, expanding industries spawned new transportation and communications systems; in turn, these systems further expanded industry, almost ensuring that America would become an industrial and economic giant.

Chapter Five

AUTOMOBILES AND THE ASSEMBLY LINE

The rise of the U.S. automobile industry was one of the great triumphs of the Industrial Revolution, both in America and worldwide. The automobile was revolutionary in many ways, but two of these stand out. First, from an industrial standpoint, it stimulated the construction of thousands of new factories and businesses and perfected the techniques of using standardized parts and long assembly lines to speed up production. Second, from a societal perspective, mass production of automobiles was a key force in changing the face of American life (and later, life in other countries) at all levels. As a noted historian of the automobile, James J. Flink, points out, the auto industry

became the backbone of a new consumer goods-oriented society . . . stimulated participation in outdoor recreation, and spurred the [construction of vast road systems and the] growth of tourism and tourism-related industries, such as service stations, roadside restaurants, and motels. . . . The automobile ended rural isolation and brought urban amenities—most important better medical care and schools—to rural America. [Also] the modern city, with its surrounding industrial and residential suburbs is a product of the automobile and trucking. . . . No other historical force has so revolutionized the way Americans work, live and play.[34]

Another significant aspect of the emergence of the U.S. auto industry was that it helped to cement and further expand America's status as the world's industrial leader. Back in the 1820s, the U.S. economy had been only a third the

The development of the assembly line in car manufacturing caused American industrial output to skyrocket.

size of Britain's, a third the size of France's, and half the size of Germany's. But by 1870, the U.S. economy had surpassed those of France and Germany and was almost equal to Britain's. By 1913, with the infant U.S. auto industry expanding, America's economy was twice that of Britain and almost four times that of France. The United States was destined to outdo Europe in auto production, along with overall industrial output, for several reasons, Flink says.

> With its vast land area and a hinterland [frontier] of scattered and isolated settlements, the United States had a far greater need for automotive transportation than the nations of Europe. Great demand was ensured, too, by a significantly higher per capita income and more equitable income distribution than in European countries. Given the American manufacturing tradition [of ingenuity, industrious workers, and large-scale markets] it was also inevitable that cars would be produced in larger volume and at lower prices than in Europe.[35]

Early Autos

It is difficult to pinpoint who built the first machine that people today would classify as an automobile, or car, and when this occurred. Some historians suggest it was a self-propelled vehicle built by French inventor Nicolas Cugnot (1725–1804) in the early 1770s. Weighing more than 2 tons (1.8 metric tons), it had three wheels, two in back and one in front. A massive steam boiler rose above the front wheel. Although this device did carry Cugnot short distances, it was not very practical. The boiler had to be relit every ten to fifteen minutes; also, the vehicle was so unbalanced and hard to steer that one day it crashed into a brick wall. Partly because of these drawbacks, Cugnot's steam carriage was abandoned and never marketed to the public.

A century passed before any major attempts were made to create self-propelled passenger vehicles, or automobiles. Strictly from a mechanical, industrial standpoint, these attempts were a direct outgrowth of the internal combustion engine; its ability to burn what were then cheap fuels like gasoline made it a pivotal industrial development. However, historians point out that a much simpler machine—the bicycle—played an equal, if not greater, role in spurring automobile development. The bicycle, which became widely popular in the 1880s and 1890s, gave Americans more freedom and desire to travel than they had experienced before and stimulated new road construction. "We could have built

The popularity of bicycles in the late nineteenth century created a demand for even faster modes of transportation.

steam[-powered autos] in 1880, or indeed in 1870," an early automaker declared,

> but we did not. We waited until 1895. The reason we did not build road vehicles before this . . . was because the bicycle had not yet come in numbers and had not directed men's minds to the possibilities of independent long-distance travel over the ordinary highway. We thought the railroad was good enough. [But] the bicycle created a new demand which it was beyond the ability of the railroad to supply. Then it came about that the bicycle could not satisfy the demand which it had created.[36]

To meet that powerful new demand for inexpensive personal transportation, several bicycle makers, along with other inventors, began focusing on the internal combustion engine. In simple terms, it works by igniting gasoline or some other liquid fuel, creating a small explosion. In turn, this pushes a piston lodged inside a cylinder. The piston's movement is transferred mechanically to two axles to which the vehicle's wheels are attached. The axles cause the wheels to turn and the car moves.

The first significant experiments with such engines took place in Belgium, France, and Germany between 1858 and 1890. Particularly noteworthy was an engine designed by German inventor Gottlieb Daimler (1834–1900) in 1885. Though crude compared to later versions, Daimler's engine worked well enough to make a bicycle move, resulting in the world's first motorcycle.

Experiments by Daimler and others directly inspired American inventors and mechanics. In 1889 two Connecticut bicycle makers, Charles E. Duryea (1861–1938) and his brother J. Frank Duryea (1869–1967) began building an auto powered by a gasoline engine. They finished and tested the vehicle in 1893, in their small way launching the automobile industry in America. Other Americans, including Elwood P. Haynes and Henry Ford, immediately began building their own autos. But the Duryea brothers managed to maintain their lead for a while by establishing the first American auto manufacturing company—the Duryea Motor Wagon Company—between 1895 and 1896. During their first year of operation, they built thirteen nearly identical vehicles.

The Rise of Big Auto Companies

At this point it was clear to many in industrial and business circles that such vehicles were on the verge of transforming the transportation industry and other aspects of American life. Among them was renowned inventor Thomas A. Edison, whose achievements in the electrical field had already given industry a hefty push forward. "The horseless vehicle is the coming wonder," he told a newspaper reporter. "It is only a question of time when the carriages and trucks in

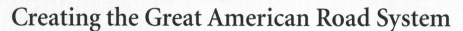

Creating the Great American Road System

One of the most important by-products of the rise of the U.S. automobile industry was a decades-long flurry of road building and road improvement to accommodate motor vehicles. Back in the 1880s, bicycle organizations, including the League of American Wheelmen, had lobbied for better road systems. But the government did not seriously consider building them until 1903. That year a convention was held in St. Louis for road-building promoters, a meeting attended by President Theodore Roosevelt. Soon, twenty-five states passed legislation to create new roads and improve older ones. With hundreds of thousands of autos pouring off assembly lines, in 1916 the federal government passed the Road Aid Act, which directed each state to create a highway department. Not long afterward, Oregon became the first state to tax gasoline to help pay for roads. In these ways, the country began creating a road system that would eventually encompass 160,000 miles (256,000km) of national and interstate highways and hundreds of thousands of miles of secondary roads.

every large city will be run with motors."[37]

The clamor to get in on the ground floor of the emerging auto industry was so great that by 1899 no less than thirty auto manufacturers were in business in the United States. That year they produced a total of 2,500 cars, a large number when one considers that each was individually crafted by hand. One of the biggest of these early companies was the Winton Motor Carriage Company in Cleveland, Ohio. It was making a then-impressive six cars a day in 1902.

Winton's location in Ohio was no accident. Most of the early New England auto companies experimented with steam and electricity for power. And when these approaches proved both impractical and too expensive, they went out of business. Most auto companies in the upper Midwest, by contrast, stuck with the more practical gasoline engine, so that region became the center of the emerging car industry. Michigan, and in particular the city of Detroit, expanded and prospered as major auto companies grew up there. By 1904 Michigan had twenty-two auto companies, most in Detroit, which together produced 42 percent of the country's cars.

Among the major auto companies that emerged during this period were the Cadillac Motor Car Company (1902), the Ford Motor Company (1903), the Buick Motor Car Company (1903), and the Olds Motor Vehicle Company (1897). Of these, Olds, owned by industrialist Ransom E. Olds (1864–1950), was initially the most successful. His chief product, the so-called Oldsmobile, was a lightweight, inexpensive, and handsome vehicle that averaged a then-respectable 14 miles per hour (22.5km/h) on the open road. Olds made twenty-four hundred of them in 1902 and four thousand in 1903. The latter number represented more than a third of all the autos sold in the United States that year.

Other companies began building appealing vehicles like the Oldsmobile, and these became so popular with the public that the industry rapidly expanded. An incredible five hundred auto companies emerged in America between 1900 and 1908. Yet the major ones could not keep up with demand. One rich investor in

One of the major auto companies to emerge during the Industrial Revolution, the Olds Motor Vehicle Company was the most successful initially. Shown here is the 1902 Oldsmobile. Olds made twenty-four hundred of these vehicles in 1902 and four thousand in 1903.

the industry remarked, "Every factory here [in Detroit] has its entire output sold and cannot begin to fill orders!"[38] Trying to fill these orders, carmakers turned out an impressive 187,000 vehicles between 1900 and 1910.

Ford and the Model T

Yet even that number, large for its time, soon paled in comparison to the output of cars by a single company. It was Ford, founded and run by Henry Ford (1863–1947), who became one of the giants of American industry and one of the richest and most successful businessmen in the world. Born a Michigan farm boy, he showed a high mechanical aptitude and became a machinist. Later he became an engineer for one of Thomas Edison's electrical companies. While working for Edison, Ford tinkered with auto engines and began building his own cars by hand.

Eventually, Ford saw a future for himself as an automaker. He quit his job with Edison and started his own company, which introduced its Model N in 1906. A statement Ford made that year to the

The Ford Motor Company was able to make and sell an astonishing number of Model T cars as a result of mass production and its creation of the assembly line.

Detroit Journal ably summed up his philosophy as a carmaker: "I believe that I have solved the problem of cheap as well as simple automobile construction. . . . The public is interested only in the knowledge that a serviceable machine can be constructed at a price within the reach of many."[39]

The Model N was a very "serviceable machine." But Ford's more advanced version, the Model T, which appeared two years later, was even more appealing. It

Ford's Controversial Treatment of Employees

One reason that Henry Ford became widely popular among Americans in the early 1900s was that he was seen as a fair, even benevolent employer. His treatment of his workers included high wages and company benefits. Among the latter were medical compensation and bonuses, including a large Christmas bonus for each worker. In 1914 Ford made news by upping his workers' pay to five dollars per day, then double the industry average. Some businessmen criticized the move, but the general public heaped praises on him. In his own defense, he later wrote in his autobiography:

The payment of high wages fortunately contributes to the low costs [of production] because the [workers] become steadily more efficient on account of being relieved of outside worries. The payment of five dollars a day for an eight-hour day was one of the finest cost-cutting moves we ever made.

Henry Ford, My Life and Work. Fairfield, IA: 1st World, 2004, p. 172.

Henry Ford was considered a fair employer who treated his workers well.

turned out to be an extremely user-friendly car that captured the interest and met the needs of large numbers of Americans. "The four-cylinder, twenty-horsepower Model T sold for $825," Flink says.

Its two-speed planetary transmission made it easy to drive, and features such as a detachable cylinder head made it easy to repair. Its high chassis was designed to clear the bumps in rural roads. [High-grade] steel made the Model T a lighter and tougher car, and new methods of casting parts . . . helped keep the price down.[40]

The Model T, also called the Tin Lizzie, was such a sensation that Ford sold ten thousand cars in its first year on the market, 1908. An amazing eighteen thousand sold in the following year. Moreover, high sales volume and more efficient production methods allowed Ford to reduce the price to $575 by 1912, making the vehicle even more popular.

Mass Production

Ford's tremendous success was due in part to his grasp of the fact that making large numbers of inexpensive autos required new and better production methods. Some other car companies had

The Laborsaving Electric Starter

One of the more important devices developed for early automobiles was the electric starter. Invented between 1911 and 1912 by noted electrical engineer Charles F. Kettering (1856–1958), it solved the problem of getting the car's motor started, which had long been a difficult chore. According to a spokesperson for the Franklin Institute:

Up to that time, automobiles were started by hand cranking, a process requiring strength and reflexes. The strength was needed to turn the hand crank connected to the large flywheel and so move the crankshaft and set the engine parts in motion. Quick reflexes were necessary for the operator to step aside immediately once the engine started and avoid the dangerous and powerful "kick back" on the turning handle when the engine started and threw off the need for the crank. Henry Leland, head of the Cadillac Motor Co., had lost a friend who was injured and later died from such a "kick back." As soon as it was available, he included the new electric starter in all Cadillac models.

Franklin Institute, "Electric Starter." www.fi.edu/learn/case-files/kettering/starter.html.

experimented in a limited way with standardized parts and division of labor (one person specializing in a single action, repeated over and over). But the typical auto was still made by a small team that assembled it bit by bit in a workshop or a fixed space on a factory floor. Each car was therefore unique and not quite identical to the others made by the same company. In contrast, Henry Ford visualized the very different outcome that would occur with more organized mass production. "The way to make automobiles," he said,

is to make one automobile just like another automobile, to make them all alike, to make them come through the factory alike. Just like one pin is like another pin when it comes from the pin factory, or one match is like another match when it comes from the match factory.[41]

To make this sort of large-scale mass production possible, Ford built a new factory in Highland Park, Michigan, in 1910. Not long afterward, he and his assistants designed a vast assembly line in which ropes attached to winches pulled each car through the plant. The pace of that motion was slow enough for a specialized worker to install one item (such as an axle, a wheel, or a headlight) before the car moved on to the next worker. One Ford company executive described it as the practice of moving the work from one worker to another until it became a complete unit, then arranging the flow of these units at the right time and the right place to a moving final assembly line from which came a finished product.[42]

The results of this new, more efficient approach to assembling autos were spectacular. In 1916 alone, Ford made and sold 739,000 Model Ts, accounting for fully one half of all new cars manufactured in the United States. And each succeeding year thereafter witnessed similar numbers. By 1927, when the company stopped making Model Ts, more than 15 million of them had been sold, an extraordinary success story even by modern standards. Ford's auto had "opened the American landscape," historian Douglas Brinkley writes, "altered the outlook of consumers everywhere, and forever changed the way automobiles [and many other products] would be manufactured and sold."[43]

The dramatic impact of Ford's achievement, and of the infant American auto industry in general, could be seen in a letter he received from a Georgia woman in 1918. "Your car lifted us out of the mud," she said. "It brought joy into our lives."[44] These words represented only one of countless examples of how the U.S. Industrial Revolution reached ever outward like a giant hand and raised the standard of living of the country's citizens.

Chapter Six

Iron, Steel, and Engineering

Americans used both iron and steel (a harder, stronger alloy of iron and carbon) in small amounts during early colonial days. Small-scale iron industries arose in the colonies, but most of the iron produced was sent to Britain. It was not until the mid-1800s that a large-scale iron industry developed in the now independent United States and began to challenge Britain's iron industry. And it was not until about 1870 that the U.S. steel industry began expanding rapidly.

These developments made the United States the global leader in both the yearly output of these metals and scientific advances related to their production. Steel proved to be particularly important because it was more versatile and more reliable than iron. According to historian John P. Hoerr:

The beginning of the 1870s was precisely the right time in the industrial development of the United States for the appearance of a steel industry. Iron had served its purpose in the early stages of the Industrial Revolution, but the infrastructure for the next great leap—railroads, bridges, factories, and office buildings—required a stronger, less malleable [bendable] material.[45]

By the 1890s U.S. steel production had surpassed that of Britain, and American steel mills turned out almost half of all the steel made in the world. As Hoerr points out, much of this steel was used to build monumental engineering projects. Huge bridges, including the renowned Brooklyn Bridge, were erected over major rivers; meanwhile, the world's first skyscrapers rose high above the streets and houses of America's big

Carnegie steel mills are pictured here in 1905. By the end of the nineteenth century, the United States had surpassed Britain in steel production.

Iron, Steel, and Engineering   65

cities. These towering edifices became new symbols of the ongoing Industrial Revolution as well as signs of America's emerging economic might.

Early American Ironworks

The earliest American ironworkers could scarcely have dreamed of these enormous future developments in their industry. These men were British ironsmiths (or blacksmiths) who crossed the Atlantic with other would-be settlers and set up workshops (often called ironworks or mills) in the newly established colonies. The first such ironwork (consisting of a large workshop) was built in the Jamestown colony in Virginia in 1621. Another emerged in Lynn, Massachusetts, in 1646; however, as this was still a tiny industry in America, the Lynn mill was unable to turn a profit and soon closed down.

These and other early ironworks typically produced two kinds of products. The smaller consisted of mundane metal items used locally, such as stoves, farming tools, and nails. The larger product was pig iron (which is somewhat brittle because it contains impurities). Most of this was shipped back to Britain to be used as a raw material in British ironworks. Very little steel was produced because at the time it was considerably more difficult and expensive to make than iron.

In 1750 the British Parliament ensured that this situation would continue by passing the Iron Act. It limited the

amount of iron products the colonists could make for themselves and mandated that most supplies be sent to Britain. Most colonists resented this law. By the mid-1700s, the thirteen American colonies were producing about a fifth of the world's raw iron. The colonists increasingly felt that they should be able to use the bulk of it for their own purposes.

Men engaged in the puddling process in the production of iron, ca. 1860. The puddling process was invented by Henry Cort to burn off impurities in the iron.

As a result, the issue became one of a series of grievances that eventually led to colonial unrest, the American Revolution, and the creation of the United States.

After the new country had formed, America had access to all its native iron supplies. However, it still lagged far behind Britain in iron production. This was largely because the already formidable

British Industrial Revolution gained momentum in the late 1700s and early 1800s. New iron-making techniques developed in Britain, whereas American ironsmiths continued to employ traditional methods. These included placing iron ore in large pans or in furnaces along with charcoal (produced by burning wood). Once the iron had partially melted, the smiths could bend or hammer it into various desired shapes. In the 1700s British ironworkers replaced the charcoal with coke, a pure form of coal that burns considerably hotter than charcoal and produces better-quality iron. As long as the Americans kept using charcoal and failed to adopt other new methods, they had no chance of seriously competing with the British in iron production.

British Advances Transform the Industry

This superiority of British iron production became clearer than ever in the half century following the American Revolution. During these years British inventors and ironworkers introduced a series of new processes that helped Britain maintain its industrial lead. The first of these new processes was called iron puddling, invented by Englishman Henry Cort (1740–1800) in the 1780s. He realized that even iron made with coke contained several impurities, including phosphorus, silica, and sulfur. These made the iron weaker and less reliable. In the puddling process, workers stirred the molten iron with long rods, causing many of the impurities to burn off. Cort also introduced a method called iron rolling. Essentially, it squeezed the puddled iron in a big press, thereby removing still more impurities.

These new processes allowed British ironworkers to produce higher-quality iron much faster than they could before. So Britain's iron industry quickly expanded during the 1790s and early 1800s. Shortly before 1750, Britain had made 23,000 tons (20,865 metric tons) of iron per year. By the 1850s, it produced 3.5 million tons (3.2 million metric tons) per year, then seen as a staggering amount. Because better-quality iron could be made faster and cheaper, people found many uses for it, including steam engines and other machines for factories, railroad tracks, bridges, barges, and cannons and other weapons.

During these same years, still another new improvement transformed Britain's iron industry—the hot-blast furnace. For a long time ironworkers had used blasts of air at room temperature (usually from bellows) to make the coke in furnaces burn hotter. In 1828 Scottish inventor James B. Neilson (1792–1865) showed that employing preheated air increased the temperature of the coke; it also reduced the amount of fuel needed in the smelting process. The iron made this way was stronger than any of the versions made before.

Eventually, American ironworkers decided that they must adopt these British methods or else continue to fall behind.

In 1830, for example, the United States produced 200,000 tons (181,437 metric tons) of iron; that same year Britain produced 700,000 tons (645,029 metric tons) of iron, mostly of better quality. In the 1830s, therefore, American iron mills, which were still small-scale outfits, began using coke rather than charcoal on a large scale; soon afterward, most of these mills adopted iron rolling and other tried-and-true British techniques. In addition, by the 1850s a lot more money was being invested in the American iron industry. As scholar Paul F. Paskoff explains, big iron companies began to emerge in response to

the [huge] requirements for capital [money] and organizational control over production imposed by the U.S. railroad industry's demand for rolled iron products, especially rails and boiler iron. Production on the scale necessary to serve the railroad's appetite for large quantities of iron at prices competitive with those charged by British producers [could only be financed by big companies].[46]

Expanding Steel Production

Yet the rising iron industry in the United States was very soon eclipsed by the domestic steel industry. Once again, the main advances triggering this transformation in America came from British and other European industries. Because high-quality steel was still quite difficult and expensive to make in large quantities, even the British took a long time to solve these problems. By 1840, for instance, Britain was producing just 80,000 tons (72,575 metric tons) of steel per year, less than a fortieth of the country's total iron industry. The growing problem was that iron, though stronger than wood and most ordinary metals, was still not strong enough to make bridges and railroad tracks completely reliable. Bridge collapses and train derailments happened fairly regularly, which people increasingly found unacceptable.

Appalled by this situation, English engineer and inventor Henry Bessemer (1813–1898) dedicated himself to finding a way to make large quantities of steel inexpensively to replace much of the iron then in use. In 1856 he unveiled a device that came to be known as the Bessemer converter. A large oval-shaped steel container, it worked by forcing streams of compressed air into molten iron until the amount of carbon in the iron reached the desired, optimal level. The process was quick and produced a great deal of high-quality steel at a reasonable price.

Less than a decade later a German engineer, Karl W. Siemens (1823–1883), and Frenchman Pierre-Émile Martin (1824–1915) perfected another steel-making process. It became known as the Siemens-Martin process in their honor. It also came to be called the open-hearth process because it employed a spacious brick chamber capable of holding hundreds of tons of iron.

A Bessemer converter in a steel factory in Pittsburgh, Pennsylvania. The Bessemer converter was invented by Henry Bessemer as a way to make large amounts of steel inexpensively.

The British Crucible Process

The emergence of large iron and steel industries in the United States owed much to a number of industrial breakthroughs of the British Industrial Revolution. One of the earliest of these took place in 1740, when English inventor Benjamin Huntsman (1704–1776) introduced the crucible process. Its name came from its use of small clay containers called crucibles. Working in his iron mill on the outskirts of Sheffield, located in central England, he put some iron in ten to twelve crucibles, then placed the crucibles in a furnace fueled by coke. When heated to high temperatures, the containers produced a modest quantity of steel. The new process stimulated steel production in Britain, which went from a total of about 200 tons (181 metric tons) a year in 1740 to more than 80,000 tons (72,575 metric tons) a year in 1840. During this period, Sheffield became the chief British steel town and one of the world's major industrial cities.

These new methods revolutionized the iron and steel industries, not only in Britain and other parts of Europe but also in the United States. The first Bessemer converter in America went into operation in 1864, at the height of the Civil War. And the first U.S. open-hearth steel mill opened four years later. Others like them appeared in rapid succession in the years that followed, as the center of the industry increasingly shifted from eastern regions, especially Pennsylvania, to the upper Midwest. "The abundance of rich iron ore around Lake Superior," scholar John S. Gordon says,

and the cheap water transport available on the Great Lakes ensured that this area would be the center of the American iron and steel industry thereafter. As the production of iron and steel became the driving force of the Industrial Revolution, the Midwest became the center of American heavy industry [eventually including auto manufacturing].[47]

As a result of these developments, American steel production expanded with remarkable swiftness. In 1860, shortly before the first Bessemer converter was installed in the United States, the country turned out only 12,000 tons (10,886 metric tons) of steel (compared to 920,000 tons, or 834,610 metric tons, of iron that year). In 1870 America produced 42,000 tons (38,102 metric tons) of steel; in 1880 about 1 million tons (907,185 metric tons); in 1890, 4.3 million tons (3.9 million metric tons), sur-

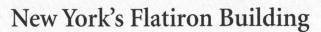

New York's Flatiron Building

New York City's leading architectural historian, Christopher Gray, wrote this informative overview of one of the first American "skyscrapers," the triangular Flatiron Building.

Although its shape is distinctive, the Flatiron Building was not praised for its architecture when it opened in 1902, nor was it advanced in its structural de-

sign. But it did represent new developments in skyscraper financing and construction practices. Popular mythology holds that the 20-story building was named by New Yorkers who scoffed at its unwieldy shape. But the triangular plot bounded by Broadway, Fifth Avenue and 22nd and 23rd Streets had been known as the "'Flat Iron" for years. . . . The Flatiron Building's triangular steel frame was also not particularly innovative, although the engineers, Purdy & Henderson, had to allow for greater than average wind bracing because the building was fairly narrow and had less bulk to provide wind resistance. . . . [One] critic [called] the design a lost opportunity. . . . But in terms of real estate development, the Flatiron represented a new age, where an insular world of New York developers was challenged by out-of-town investors, attracted by the great profits available here in single bursts of skyscraper construction.

Christopher Gray, "From Flat Iron to Flatiron," Tom Fletcher's New York Architecture Images and Notes. www.nyc-architecture.com/GRP/GRP024.htm.

The Flatiron Building in New York was one of America's first skyscrapers.

passing Britain, which made just 700,000 tons (635,029 metric tons) that year; in 1900, 10 million tons (9.1 million metric tons); and in 1910, 24 million tons (22 million metric tons).

Steel for Great Engineering Projects

Now that builders and engineers had access to large amounts of strong, reliable steel at affordable prices, they began employing more and more steel in large-scale structures. Moreover, with the stability steel provided, such structures could be built considerably bigger than in the past. Bridges, for example, could be both longer and higher. One of the first major triumphs in the new wave of bridge building was the Eads Bridge, spanning the Mississippi River at St. Louis. Designed by American engineer James B. Eads (1820–1887), it was completed in 1874. It was 6,442 feet (1,964m) long, which made it at the time the longest arched bridge in the world. Eads used large quantities of high-grade steel, along with lesser amounts of high-quality iron, and his use of ribbed steel arches for support was then viewed as daring.

Even more impressive, as well as more famous, was the Brooklyn Bridge, which

The development of the steel industry spurred the creation of large-scale construction projects, such as the construction of the Brooklyn Bridge.

The Historic Woolworth Building

Another of the early American skyscrapers made possible by structural steel frames was New York City's Woolworth Building. Completed in 1913 and designed by architect Cass Gilbert (1859–1934), it has often been called the first true skyscraper because at a height of 792 feet (241m) it towered over earlier so-called skyscrapers. In an attempt to give the structure a Gothic look (like a number of medieval European cathedrals), Gilbert erected a Gothic-style tower on top of the building's rectangular lower half. Though the Woolworth Building was and remains an office building, its similarity to a Gothic cathedral has prompted some people to call it a "cathedral of commerce." The structure, now listed as an American historic landmark, remained the tallest building in the world until 40 Wall Street and the Chrysler Building were built between 1929 and 1930.

The Woolworth Building has been called the first true skyscraper because of its great height.

crosses the East River to connect New York's communities of Manhattan and Brooklyn. By the 1840s the locals were desperate for a safe, easy, and speedy way to cross the river. Ferries had long been used but were slow and sometimes sank in the strong currents. "The only thing to be thought of is a bridge,"[48] the *New York Tribune* stated in 1849. But such a bridge would need to be enormous, and at the time no one possessed either the expertise or strong enough materials to do the job.

By the late 1860s, however, the situation had changed dramatically. Large amounts of steel were now available. And a brilliant German-born American engineer named John A. Roebling (1806–1869) came forward with a bold design for a huge suspension bridge. In a suspension bridge, the road and walkways are suspended from cables strung across two or more upright support towers. Roebling died unexpectedly shortly before construction began in 1870. But his son, Washington A. Roebling (1837–1926), also a skilled engineer, took over the project. It was completed in 1883 and immediately became a symbol and testament to American industrial might as well as American ingenuity and boldness. Indeed, Americans were "thrilled with the Brooklyn Bridge," Deborah Cadbury writes. They were

in love with the sheer American audacity of the enterprise. [It] had become the eighth wonder of the world. People jumped from it, fell in love on it, married on it, someone even took a herd of elephants over it; and by 1888, 30 million passengers a year took the train over it.[49]

American-made steel also went into building the skeletons of tremendous new buildings that came to be called skyscrapers. The first, erected in Chicago in 1885, was the Home Insurance Company Building, designed by William LeBaron Jenney (1832–1907). It was small by today's standards—at ten stories and 138 feet (42m). But it paved the way for much taller buildings, including New York's Flatiron Building ([1902], 285 feet, or 87m); Chicago's Masonic Temple ([1892], 302 feet, or 92m); New York's Woolworth Building ([1913], 792 feet, or 241m); New York's Chrysler Building ([1930], 1,045 feet, or 319m); and New York's Empire State Building ([1931], 1,250 feet, or 381m). Many people, including numerous foreigners, looked at these massive engineering projects in awe. They saw them as proof that America's Industrial Revolution had made it the strongest, cleverest, richest, and most enviable nation on Earth.

Chapter Seven

THE ONSET OF INDUSTRIALIZED WARFARE

During the middle to late 1800s and early 1900s, the American Industrial Revolution won the world's admiration for the factories, steel mills, railroad systems, towering bridges and skyscrapers, and other technological achievements. All of these were seen as examples of progress in American and human society. However, the onrush of industry and technology also had darker sides that were far from progressive and were often destructive.

Among these was the rise of industrialized warfare. Scattered advances in mechanized weaponry occurred both in Europe and the United States during the early to middle 1800s. But it was in the United States, during and immediately following the Civil War, that such advances began to emerge in a systematic way and on an increasingly larger scale. For this reason, that conflict, fought be-

tween 1861 and 1865, is frequently referred to as the first modern war. The technological developments industry had recently produced certainly made it an exceedingly lethal and bloody war. More than 623,000 soldiers lost their lives, and at least 100,000 civilians were killed. These losses were greater than those sustained by Americans in the American Revolution, the War of 1812, the Mexican-American War, the Spanish-American War, World War I, World War II, and the Korean War combined.

After the war ended, the arms industries continued to expand and turn out still more deadly weapons. Moreover, Britain, France, Germany, Japan, and other nations created or enlarged their own military-industrial complexes, spawning a ferocious modern arms race. It soon culminated in the largest, most destructive conflict humanity had yet endured—World War I. Fought from 1914 to 1918, at the height of America's Industrial Revolution, it was the first war to apply mechanized weapons, many of U.S. invention, on a nearly global scale.

The Stirrings of Mechanized Warfare

Before the Industrial Revolution, technological advances in weaponry, transportation, and communication occurred fairly slowly, over the course of many centuries. The main weapons had long included swords; spears; crude and inaccurate handheld guns (including the muskets used in the American Revolution and the War of 1812, which required that a lead ball and gunpowder be reloaded by hand after each shot); rudimentary cannons; and old-fashioned sailing ships. On land, troops traveled on foot or by horse, and war communications were carried by messengers on horseback.

Making More Guns

The application of the factory concepts of division of labor and mass production to gun manufacturing significantly changed

A Civil War cemetery in Alexandria, Virginia. The development of more sophisticated weapons around the time of the war made it the bloodiest conflict in American history.

President Abraham Lincoln tests the Spencer repeater in 1863, which fired up to twenty rounds per minute.

this situation. In 1798 Eli Whitney, who had earlier invented the cotton gin, was awarded a U.S. government contract to produce between ten and fifteen thousand muskets. In the years that followed, he built a factory in Mill Rock, Connecticut. There he trained his workers to create interchangeable parts for gun assembly; this was much more efficient than each gunsmith fabricating parts that did not match those of other gunsmiths. Also, instead of a single person assembling an entire gun, Whitney's employees each concentrated on one or two specialized assembly tasks. This new approach, which became known as the American system, was adopted by government armories, including the major one in Springfield, Massachusetts. The Springfield Armory increased production by 1,000 percent between the 1840s and the 1860s.

Making Guns More Lethal

During these same years, gunsmiths were hard at work trying both to improve the efficiency of muskets and to create other handheld guns that were more accurate and lethal than muskets. The most significant of these weapons, the rifle, started to replace the musket just prior to the Civil War. The term *rifle* refers to "rifling," a set of spiral grooves on the inside of the gun's barrel. (The inside of a musket's barrel was smooth.) After someone fired a rifle, the bullet moved through the grooves and departed the gun spinning; this produced a shot that could travel a greater distance with more accuracy.

One reason why rifles did not immediately replace muskets was because early rifles required more time to load than most muskets. The main problem was that a bullet small enough for the rifleman to insert easily into the barrel would be too small to fit into the grooves. The ideal solution was to find a small bullet that expanded in size at the right moment. This solution came in the late 1840s when a French soldier, Claude-Étienne Minié, invented the so-called minié ball. It "had a hollow base with an iron plug inserted," military historian Ian Drury explains. "The moment the rifle was fired, the bullet expanded. The hard iron plug was driven violently into the softer lead, forcing it against the sides of the barrel as it raced toward the muzzle."[50]

Also, weapons designers made the firepower of a rifle more formidable by increasing the number of bullets it could fire in a single reload. The repeating rifle, or "repeater," used cartridges containing multiple bullets, each of which entered the firing chamber automatically. Particularly effective was the Spencer repeater, named after its inventor, Christopher M. Spencer (1833–1922), of Connecticut. It fired up to twenty rounds per minute, making it an unprecedented killing machine for its time.

Machine Guns and Artillery

Though effective and deadly, such repeaters were no match for the first so-called machine guns (the term *machine* being an obvious reference to their industrial origins).

A single-barreled, hand-cranked version, the Williams machine gun, appeared during the Civil War. More complex and lethal was the Gatling gun, introduced by Richard J. Gatling (1818–1903) of North Carolina in 1861. It had six separate barrels that rotated and fired in succession. More advanced versions were created by American and French inventors during the next two decades, culminating in 1885 with a single-barrel gun invented by Hiram Maxim (1840–1916) of Maine. It fired ten rounds per second, then viewed as both phenomenal and frightening.

Cannons, more properly termed *artillery*, also underwent rapid industrial advancement during the late 1800s. Some cannons, then made of iron, had become rifled, increasing their accuracy and range, by the time of the Civil War. Lighter, more mobile cannons were employed against foot soldiers during that conflict. In July 1862, for example, at Malvern Hill, Virginia, Union artillery fired into attacking waves of Confederate troops, killing more than five thousand. In the words of shaken Confederate general D.H. Hill, "It was not war—it was murder."[51]

In the decades following the Civil War, still more advances in artillery took place. These included steel cannons that fired ten shells per minute as far as 3 miles (4.8km), which was five times farther than the versions used in the Civil War; smokeless powder, which made it easier for artillery gunners to see their

Early Machine Guns

By today's standards, early American-made machine guns were crude. Because they had to be cranked by hand, it might be more accurate to call them mechanically operated repeaters. Another drawback was that they used charges of gunpowder, causing residue to build up and lessen their effectiveness. The most widely used of these devices was the Williams machine gun, invented by a Confederate officer. Military historian Ian Drury tells how it worked.

Self-consuming paper cartridges [each filled with gunpowder] were fed into the breech by hand and a percussion cap was placed on a nipple to the left of the chamber. The gun was operated by a crank and connecting rod that forced the breech block back and forth. By moving the crank the breech block was moved forward, chambering the cartridge and tripping the hammer. As the block came back, the hammer rose clear of the nipple once more and the process was repeated.

Ian Drury and Tony Gibbons, *The Civil War Military Machine: Weapons and Tactics of the Union and Confederate Armed Forces.* New York: Smithmark, 1993, p. 64.

The Gatling gun was a lethal machine gun that consisted of six separate barrels that rotated and fired in succession.

New inventions and industrial processes also led to advancements in naval warfare. Metal-plated warships appeared in the Civil War where the Virginia *(left) and the* Monitor *met in battle near Hampton Roads, Virginia.*

targets and aim; and shells having more explosive power than earlier versions.

Advanced Naval Weaponry

Major advances also occurred in naval warfare as a result of American and other Western inventors and the new industrial processes they engineered. One such advance consisted of onboard artillery that fired large explosive shells instead of simple cannonballs. The terrible damage such shells could do became clear in 1853, when six Russian warships used them to destroy nearly an entire Turkish fleet of wooden sailing ships in the Black Sea.

Even more pivotal was the introduction of metal-plated warships designed to counter such shells. The earliest examples, then called ironclads, appeared in the American Civil War. In 1861 Confederate naval engineers covered a wooden warship, the *Merrimack,* with more than 800 tons (726 metric tons) of iron plates. Renamed the *Virginia,* it met the first Union ironclad, the *Monitor,* in battle near Hampton Roads, Virginia, early in 1862.

During the four-hour encounter, the lighter *Monitor* consistently outmaneuvered the other ship. No matter how hard they tried, however, neither vessel was able to damage the other in any major way. One of the *Monitor's* officers later wrote:

Five times during the engagement we touched each other, and each time I fired a gun at her. . . . Once she tried to run us down with her iron prow but did no damage whatever. . . . [We attacked her] as hard as we could, the shot, shell, grape, canister, musket, and rifle balls flying in every direction but doing no damage. Our tower was struck several times . . . [but] it did not affect us any.[52]

This historic battle showed that armorplated ships were the wave of future naval warfare. And indeed, the naval arms race that followed produced larger and larger metal warships, now called battleships, weighing from 10,000 to 15,000 tons (9,072 to 13,608 metric tons), some five times more than the largest traditional wooden warships.

During the Civil War, a young engineer from Charleston, South Carolina, Francis D. Lee (1826–1885), invented the "spar torpedo," essentially a can of gunpowder attached to a long pole. To deliver this weapon, the Confederacy created several new warships with spar torpedoes extending forward from their bows. The goal was to ram and blow up enemy ships.

In addition to these above-water vessels, the Confederates created the first effective submarine to deliver the torpedoes below the waterline. The *Hunely,* named for its builder, Horace L. Hunely (1823–1863), consisted of an iron cylinder 20 feet (6m) long and 5 feet (1.5m) wide with a metal shaft that spun the propeller. On February 17, 1864, the vessel successfully sank the USS *Housatonic* near Charleston. But the blast also destroyed the sub.

Experiments with submersibles continued in the years that followed. Much more effective submarines were perfected by 1914, the year World War I began. These vessels weighed several hundred tons and carried about a dozen torpedoes, which were used with horrific effect. In 1916 German submarines alone sank more than 2.2 million tons (2 million metric tons) of shipping.

Increasing the Scope of War

In addition to more advanced and deadly weapons, the American Industrial Revolution (aided to some degree by foreign inventors) developed other technological devices that increased the scope and efficiency of war. These advances were initially intended to make transportation and communications faster and easier; but their potential application to warfare quickly became apparent. For example, the Civil War was the first conflict in which railroads played a key role. Generals often took advantage of the ever-expanding networks of tracks to transport large numbers of troops by rail. Trains also routinely carried food and other supplies. Not surprisingly, each side tried to

Steamers Become Warships

Ironclads like the Monitor *were not the only warships to take advantage of new industrial materials and processes during the Civil War era. Some American naval engineers took ordinary steamships and outfitted them with sturdy rams in their bows. These ships became known as "rams" because their chief tactic was to ram and sink enemy ships. In 1862 Union engineer Charles Ellet of Pittsburgh bought nine fast steamers and reinforced the bow of each with a ram. He then moved his small fleet down the Mississippi to help several Union gunboats (small rivercraft carrying cannons) in an attack on the Confederate city of Memphis, Tennessee. In a battle fought near the city on June 6, Ellet's rams destroyed or captured all but one of the Confederate gunboats. Afterward, Ellet's brother, Alfred, said:*

The battle of Memphis was, in many respects, one of the most remarkable naval victories on record. For [our] unarmed, frail, wooden river steamboats, with barely men enough on board to handle the machinery and keep the furnace-fires burning, to rush . . . *into* the enemy's advancing line . . . was a sight never before witnessed.

Quoted in Henry S. Commager, ed., *The Blue and the Gray: The Story of the Civil War as Told by Its Participants.* New York: Bobbs-Merrill, 1950, p. 818.

seize control of vital railway connections, which led to a number of skirmishes and battles.

Another product of the industrial age, the telegraph, also became an important factor in the Civil War as well as several conflicts that immediately followed it. Commanders were able to send vital messages to distant locations almost instantly. The thousands of miles of telegraph lines strung out across the Northern states played an important role in the overall Union victory.

These and other technical advances in the waging of war continued until the outbreak of World War I, which pitted Germany, Austria-Hungary, and Turkey against France, Britain, Russia, and eventually the United States. That titanic conflict saw not only the use of artillery, machine guns, battleships, and submarines but also other new products of industrialization. These included tanks, primitive airplanes, and the telephone (which further advanced wartime communications). The war, which showcased American industrial might to the world, proved to be a watershed in the long evolution of warfare. It marked the emergence of the "technology-oriented battlefield," as military historian Christon I. Archer puts it.

No longer were moral qualities [of soldiers and nations] sufficient to win. Now it was necessary as never before to integrate technology in the form of various weapon systems into the operations of war. Technology could more easily defeat technology, rather than relying on courage and discipline to overcome machine guns and artillery.[53]

As is only too clear today, the industrial-technological arms race did not stop in 1918 at the close of the "Great War," as people then called it. Even more destructive weapons were subsequently invented and used in a series of awful conflicts, among them World War II, the Korean War, the Vietnam War, and the Iraq War that began when U.S. troops entered that country in 2003. Neither did other technical advances stop in 1918. True, the term *Industrial Revolution* was used less and less to describe such advances. Yet those that occurred in the so-called modern era were nonetheless part of the same industrial progression that began in the 1700s. So far, that era has produced machines and technologies even more influential and transforming than the ones that appeared before World War I.

Epilogue

AMERICAN INDUSTRY IN THE MODERN ERA

The twentieth century and early years of the twenty-first century witnessed unprecedented, truly monumental advances in industry and technology. The lives of people worldwide, and in particular in the United States and other Western societies, were profoundly affected by these advances. Today the citizens of these societies take for granted the ease and swiftness of transportation, communications, and the buying and selling that people in 1900 did not anticipate.

It is important to emphasize that these advances were accompanied by major alterations in the *kinds* of industrial processes and products that came to drive society and national economies. The large-scale industries that had emerged in the United States in the nineteenth century—such as textiles, railroads, and steel—remained strong until the mid-twentieth century. However, over time they declined in economic impact and influence. The number of Americans working in traditional manufacturing industries decreased from 31 to 19 percent over the course of the twentieth century.

The automobile industry remained vital longer than most of the others. Indeed, in the years following World War II, cars became a chief symbol of America's industrialized culture. "If any industry represented America's industrial might in the twentieth century," one expert observer recently noted,

surely it was auto makers. The handful of companies clustered around Detroit produced the assembly line ... tanks and aircraft engines during World War II, and thousands of high-paying factory jobs when peace came. The industry became the backbone

The invention of the computer has been one of the most influential developments of the twentieth century.

U.S. Industry and Future Warfare

In addition to automobiles, television, computers, and the Internet, the onrush of American industry and technology has produced generations of new and more lethal weapons. Among them are helicopters armed with missiles, warplanes invisible to radar, nuclear submarines, laser- and computer-guided bombs, satellites that gather intelligence about the enemy, and goggles that allow soldiers to see in the dark. American industry and technology will almost certainly play a central role in shaping the future of warfare. In the words of noted political scientists George and Meredith Friedman:

Just as the gun shaped European power and culture, it appears . . . that precision-guided munitions will shape American power and culture. Just as Europe expanded war and its power to the global oceans, the United States is expanding war and its power into space. . . . Just as Europe shaped the world for half a millennium, so too the United States will shape the world for at least that length of time. For better or worse, America has seized hold of the future of war, and with it—for a time—the future of humanity.

George Friedman and Meredith Friedman, *The Future of War: Power, Technology, and American World Dominance in the Twenty-first Century.* New York: St. Martin's Griffin, 1996, p. 420.

of the U.S. economy and its companies America's bellwethers. As cars went, so went the nation.[54]

One of the many ways the auto industry reshaped America was by stimulating the building of an enormous network of roads. By 2004 U.S. interstate highways alone totaled 46,837 miles (75,376km), the largest single highway system in the world.

The Information Age

Even larger and more influential in remaking the United States and the world, however, was a major shift in industrial and technological development toward electronics, communications, and information technologies. The spectacular evolution of the telephone represents only one of many examples. In 1904 there were about 3 million phones in the United States. By 2006 there were several hundred million, spread among businesses and private homes; in that same year there were also 4 billion phones worldwide.

Moreover, as in all modern technologies, the growth has been not only in the number of users, but also in the sophistication and versatility of the device. Cell phones, giving users unheard-of flexibility and convenience, emerged in the 1980s. In 1990 the United States had 4 million cell phones, and by 2000 it had 100 million. In addition, by 2005, 55 million U.S. cell phones were equipped with another modern electronic marvel—text messaging.

The electronic and information age of the twentieth century and beyond has produced even more far-reaching technologies and devices. Chief among them are radio, television, satellites orbiting Earth and other planets, computers, and the Internet. Of these, television has been particularly influential in reshaping society, especially in the United States, where the first large television industry developed. As a noted television historian, Anthony Smith, phrases it, television

> exercised an unanticipated and transforming influence [on America and the world]. Political life in democracies and non-democracies alike was thoroughly altered under the impact of television. A new consumer [buyer and user] society came to depend on it. . . . Television has imposed its own ways upon everyone in society who needs to communicate something to an audience. By 1990 in the developed [industrialized] world, 98 percent of homes had come to possess a television.[55]

Similarly, most homes in these countries today have computers. In the late twentieth century, computers were also installed in virtually all businesses, offices, factories, stores, restaurants, and hospitals, becoming instrumental in transactions, billing, scheduling, inventory, ordering, word processing, and much more. A technological extension of the computer, the Internet, has been no less influential and socially transforming. It has radically changed the way many people gather news and information, communicate, shop, and entertain themselves. Moreover, it is expanding and becoming more sophisticated with each passing year. In 1996 there were 300 million Internet users worldwide; by 2004, 800,000 billion; and by 2008, 1.4 billion.

A Profound Transition

The rapid spread of computers and expansion of the Internet clearly illustrate how quickly the ongoing industrial and technological revolutions are producing technical and social change. According to the legendary business management authority Peter Drucker, "We live in a period of profound transition. And changes are more radical perhaps than even those that ushered in the 'Second Industrial Revolution' of the middle of the nineteenth century."[56] As a result of this rapid, unpredictable flurry of change, experts say that it is difficult to predict how different the world will be as little as twenty or thirty years from now. One thing is certain: It will be a place of which the early British and American inventors and industrialists scarcely could have dreamed.

Notes

Introduction: The Second American Revolution

1. Steven M. Beaudoin, ed., *The Industrial Revolution*. Boston: Houghton Mifflin, 2003, p. 3.
2. Alfred D. Chandler, "Industrial Revolution," in *The Reader's Companion to American History*, ed. Eric Foner and John A. Garraty. Boston: Houghton Mifflin, 1991, p. 560.
3. John F. Kasson, "Republican Values as a Dynamic Factor," in *The Industrial Revolution in America*, ed. Gary J. Kornblith. Boston: Houghton Mifflin, 1998, p. 3.

Chapter One: The Origins of American Industry

4. Kornblith, *The Industrial Revolution in America*, p. xv.
5. Quoted in Philip B. Kurland and Ralph Lerner, eds., "Alexander Hamilton, Report on Manufactures," Founders' Constitution. http://press-pubs.uchicago.edu/founders/documents/v1ch4s31.html.
6. Laura L. Frader, *The Industrial Revolution: A History in Documents*. New York: Oxford University Press, 2006, p. 20.
7. Quoted in Laurel T. Ulrich, *A Midwife's Tale: The Life of Martha Ballard Based on Her Diary, 1785–1812*. New York: Vintage, 1991, p. 38.
8. Paul E. Rivard, *A New Order of Things: How the Textile Industry Transformed New England*. Hanover, NH: University Press of New England, 2002, p. 5.
9. E.J. Hobsbawm and Chris Wrigley, *Industry and Empire: From 1750 to the Present Day*. New York: Norton, 1999, p. xi.
10. Quoted in David Lear Buckman, "Old Steamboat Days on the Hudson River," Hudson River Maritime Museum. www.hrmm.org/diglib/old steam/chapter2.html.

Chapter Two: Textile Mills Lead the Way

11. Quoted in Moses Greenleaf, *A Survey of the State of Maine in Reference to Its Geographical Features, Statistics, and Political Economy*. Augusta, ME: Maine State Museum, 1979, p. 277.
12. Quoted in John F. Schroeder, ed., *Maxims of Washington*. New York: D. Appleton, 1894, p. 137.
13. Rivard, *A New Order of Things*, p. 11.
14. Rivard, *A New Order of Things*, p. 11.
15. Jeff Horn, *The Industrial Revolution*. Westport, CT: Greenwood, 2007, p. 37.
16. Kax Wilson, *A History of Textiles*. Boulder, CO: Westview, 1979, p. 72.

17. Rivard, *A New Order of Things,* p. 44.
18. Rivard, *A New Order of Things,* p. 46.
19. Nathan Appleton, *Introduction of the Power Loom.* Boston: B.H. Penhallow, 1858, pp. 9–10.
20. Quoted in Betina Eisler, *The Lowell Offering: Writings by New England Mill Women.* New York: Harper, 1977, p. 53.

Chapter Three: New Energy Sources for Power

21. Barbara Freese, *Coal: A Human History.* New York: Perseus, 2003, pp. 121–22.
22. Quoted in National Parks Service, "American Steam Locomotives." www .nps.gov/history/history/online_books /steamtown/shs2.htm.
23. Daniel Yergin, *The Prize: The Epic Quest for Oil, Money, and Power.* New York: Simon & Schuster, 1991, p. 7.

Chapter Four: Transportation and Communications

24. William Cronon, "Railroads and the Reorganization of Nature and Time," in Kornblith, *The Industrial Revolution in America,* p. 135.
25. Quoted in Drew R. McCoy, *The Last of the Fathers: James Madison and the Republican Legacy.* New York: Cambridge University Press, 1991, p. 94.
26. Herman Bryant, *Along the Kennebec.* Mt. Pleasant, SC: Arcadia, 1995, p. 114.

27. Horn, *The Industrial Revolution,* pp. 104–5.
28. James A. Ward, *Railroads and the Character of America, 1820–1877.* Knoxville: University of Tennessee Press, 1986, p. 61.
29. Cronon, "Railroads and the Reorganization of Nature and Time," p. 136.
30. Deborah Cadbury, *Dreams of Iron and Steel: Seven Wonders of the Nineteenth Century.* New York: Fourth Estate, 2004, p. 158.
31. Quoted in Cadbury, *Dreams of Iron and Steel,* p. 190.
32. Cadbury, *Dreams of Iron and Steel,* p. 191.
33. Colin Cherry, "The Telephone System: Creator of Mobility and Social Change," Institute for Philosophical Research, Hungarian Academy of Sciences. www.fil.hu/mobil/konyvtar/ pool/cherry.htm.

Chapter Five: Automobiles and the Assembly Line

34. James J. Flink, "Automobiles," in Foner and Garraty, *The Reader's Companion to American History,* p. 67.
35. Flink, "Automobiles," p. 65.
36. Hiram P. Maxim, *Horseless Carriage Days.* New York: Harper, 1937, pp. 4–5.
37. Quoted in James J. Flink, *America Adopts the Automobile, 1895–1910.* Cambridge, MA: MIT Press, 1970, p. 21.
38. Quoted in James J. Flink, *The Automobile Age.* Cambridge, MA: MIT Press, 1988, p. 27.

39. Quoted in Flink, *The Automobile Age,* p. 37.
40. Flink, "Automobiles," p. 65.
41. Quoted in Flink, *The Automobile Age,* p. 43.
42. Charles E. Sorensen, *My Forty Years with Ford.* New York: Norton, 1956, p. 16.
43. Douglas Brinkley, "Prime Mover." www.geocities.com/clifftyndall03/modelt.htm.
44. Quoted in Brinkley, "Prime Mover."

Chapter Six: Iron, Steel, and Engineering

45. John P. Hoerr, *And the Wolf Finally Came: The Decline of the American Steel Industry.* Pittsburgh: University of Pittsburgh Press, 1988, p. 84.
46. Paul F. Paskoff, *Industrial Evolution: Organization, Structure, and Growth of the Pennsylvania Iron Industry, 1750–1869.* Baltimore: Johns Hopkins University Press, 1983, p. 53.
47. John S. Gordon, "Iron and Steel Industry," in Foner and Garraty, *The Reader's Companion to American History,* p. 574.
48. Quoted in Cadbury, *Dreams of Iron and Steel,* p. 80.
49. Cadbury, *Dreams of Iron and Steel,* p. 114.

Chapter Seven: The Onset of Industrialized Warfare

50. Ian Drury and Tony Gibbons, *The Civil War Military Machine: Weapons and Tactics of the Union and Confederate Armed Forces.* New York: Smithmark, 1993, p. 51.
51. Quoted in Thomas B. Buell, *Combat Leadership in the Civil War.* New York: Crown, 1997, p. 89.
52. Quoted in Lydia M. Post, ed., *Soldiers' Letters from Camp, Battlefield, and Prison.* New York: Bunce and Huntington, 1865, p. 112.
53. Christon I. Archer et al., *World History of Warfare.* Lincoln: University of Nebraska Press, 2002, p. 510.

Epilogue: American Industry in the Modern Era

54. Joann Muller, "Autos: A New Industry," *Business Week,* July 15, 2002. www.businessweek.com/magazine/content/02_28/b3791001.htm.
55. Anthony Smith, ed., *Television: An International History.* New York: Oxford University Press, 1998, pp. 1–2.
56. Peter Drucker, *Management Challenges for the 21st Century.* New York: HarperCollins, pp. ix–x.

Time Line

1752
American inventor Benjamin Franklin shows that lightning is a form of electricity.

1756
The Seven Years' War begins with fighting on three different continents—Asia, Europe, and North America.

1776
England's thirteen American colonies declare their independence.

1789
French citizens storm the Bastille, officially marking the beginning of the French Revolution.

1790
The first U.S. textile mill is built on the Blackstone River in Pawtucket, Rhode Island.

1791
Thomas Paine publishes *The Rights of Man*. American founding father Alexander Hamilton calls for the building of factories in the United States.

1793
American inventor Eli Whitney patents the cotton gin.

1800
The Library of Congress is established with a budget of five thousand dollars to purchase some nine hundred books.

1807
Robert Fulton initiates steamboat service on the Hudson River.

1810
In South America, Argentina gains its independence.

1825
The Erie Canal opens, facilitating trade from the East Coast to the Ohio Valley.

1840
Transatlantic steam service between Europe and the Americas begins.

1854
U.S. admiral Matthew Perry arrives with a squadron of ships in Japan.

1859
English naturalist Charles Darwin publishes *The Origin of Species*.

1861–1865
The American Civil War is waged.

1864
Navajo Indians are forced to march 800 miles (1,287km) from their homeland to the Bosque Redondo reserve in New Mexico.

1865
The Thirteenth Amendment ends slavery in the United States.

1867
Swedish chemist and engineer Alfred Nobel invents dynamite, which revolutionizes warfare.

1870–1871
The Franco-Prussian War rocks Europe.

1881
U.S. president James Garfield is assassinated.

1883
The first skyscraper (rising ten stories) is built in Chicago; the Brooklyn Bridge is inaugurated in New York City.

1892
Large oil deposits are found in California.

1900
The United States has 193,000 miles (310,603km) of railroad tracks.

1904
The Russo-Japanese War begins as Russia and Japan vie for control of Manchuria and Korea.

1906
An earthquake rocks San Francisco and triggers a fire that lasts for three days and burns more than 4 square miles (10 sq. km.) of the city.

1914
World War I erupts in Europe.

1917
The United States joins World War I on the side of the Allies—Great Britain, France, Belgium, Italy, and Russia.

1929
The stock market crashes on October 29, triggering the beginning of the Great Depression.

For More Information

Books

Christon I. Archer et al., *World History of Warfare*. Lincoln: University of Nebraska Press, 2002. A well-informed overview of warfare, including advances in weaponry during the Industrial Revolution.

T.S. Ashton and Pat Hudson, *The Industrial Revolution, 1760–1830*. New York: Oxford University Press, 1998. An excellent general look at the early years of the Industrial Revolution. Hudson, an economic historian, provides commentary updating Ashton's classic 1949 book.

Deborah Cadbury, *Dreams of Iron and Steel: Seven Wonders of the Nineteenth Century*. New York: Fourth Estate, 2004. This book examines several megaprojects made possible by industrialization, including the Panama Canal, Brooklyn Bridge, and London's sewers.

Laura L. Frader, *The Industrial Revolution: A History in Documents*. New York: Oxford University Press, 2006. One of the best collections of primary sources for the Industrial Revolution.

Kevin Hillstrom and Laurie C. Hillstrom, eds., *Industrial Revolution in America: Automobiles*. Santa Barbara, CA: ABC-CLIO, 2006. This and the Hillstroms' other books about the Industrial Revolution (see below) are detailed and informative.

——, *Industrial Revolution in America: Communications*. Santa Barbara, CA: ABC-CLIO, 2007.

——, *Industrial Revolution in America: Iron and Steel*. Santa Barbara, CA: ABC-CLIO, 2005.

——, *Industrial Revolution in America: Railroads*. Santa Barbara, CA: ABC-CLIO, 2005.

Gary J. Kornblith, ed., *The Industrial Revolution in America*. Boston: Houghton Mifflin, 1998. This book contains a series of thought-provoking essays by assorted scholars about how the United States became an industrial giant.

Don Nardo, *History of Weapons and Warfare: The Civil War*. San Diego: Lucent, 2002. This work explains how new weapons and military technology emerging in the mid-1800s were applied to one of the century's great wars.

Paul E. Rivard, *A New Order of Things: How the Textile Industry Transformed New England*. Hanover, NH: University Press of New England, 2002. A well-written, information-packed look at the early rise of the textile industry in America.

Peter N. Stearns, *The Industrial Revolution in World History.* Boulder, CO: Westview, 2007. A good, straightforward look at the Industrial Revolution and how it changed the world.

R. Conrad Stein, *The Industrial Revolution: Manufacturing a Better America.* Berkeley Heights, NJ: Enslow, 2006. Aimed at young adult readers, this well-written book looks mainly at the emergence of industrialization in the United States.

Norman Ware, *The Industrial Worker, 1840–1860: The Reaction of American Industrial Society to the Advance of the Industrial Revolution.* Chicago: I.R. Dee, 1990. A detailed examination of how emerging industries and the factory system affected American workers.

Web Sites

The Brooklyn Bridge (www.nyc-archi tecture.com/BRI/BRI001-Brooklyn Bridge.htm). This excellent site about the great New York landmark contains many stunning photos and paintings, along with loads of information about the bridge's construction and vital statistics.

History of the Transcontinental Railroad (http://bushong.net/dawn/about /college/ids100/history.shtml). This site tells how this huge engineering and transportation project was conceived and built.

The Industrial Revolution (www.ford ham.edu/halsall/mod/modsbook14 .html). Part of the Internet Modern History Source Book, this site contains a very useful collection of articles on the Industrial Revolution, including several on its social, political, and urban effects.

The Industrial Revolution: An Overview (www.victorianweb.org/technology/ ir/irov.html). This site, which is part of the Victorian Web, has an excellent compilation of short articles on Industrial Revolution topics, including textiles, railroads, inventors, engineers, a chronology, and much more.

The Life of Henry Ford (www.thehenry ford.org/exhibits/hf). A brief but informative look at one of the founding fathers of the U.S. automobile industry.

Index

Picture Credits

Cover, the Library of Congress
© The Print Collector/Alamy, 81
© Bettmann/Corbis, 20, 38, 48, 59, 60, 70, 82-83
American School, (19th century)/Library of Congress, Washington D.C., USA/The Bridgeman Art Library, 11
American School, (19th century)/Private Collection/Peter Newark American Pictures/The Bridgeman Art Library, 18
American School, (18th century)/Smithsonian Institution, Washington D.C., USA/The Bridgeman Art Library, 27
English School, (18th century)/Musee des Beaux-Arts, Dieppe, France/Lauros/Giraudon/The Bridgeman Art Library, 16
English School, (19th century)/Private Collection/The Bridgeman Art Library, 35
Hatton Gallery, University of Newcastle Upon Tyne, UK/The Bridgeman Art Library, 33
Lampitt, Ronald (Ron) (1906-88)/Private Collection/© Look and Learn/The Bridgeman Art Library, 13
Private Collection/Avant-Demain/The Bridgeman Art Library, 56
Private Collection/© Look and Learn/The Bridgeman Art Library, 25
Private Collection/Peter Newark American Pictures/The Bridgeman Art Library, 78
© Stefano Bianchetti/Corbis, 51
Dennie Cody/Taxi/Getty Images, 77
Neil Emmerson/Robert Harding World Imagery/Getty Images, 72
Sylvain Grandadam/Robert Harding World Imagery/Getty Images, 74
Hulton Archive/Getty Images, 19, 39, 66-67
Museum of the City of New York/Getty Images, 73
Thomas Phillips/The Bridgeman Art Library/Getty Images, 41
Stock Montage/Hulton Archive/Getty Images, 61
© Mary Evans Picture Library/The Image Works, 44-45
National Archives and Records Administration, 15
© North Wind Picture Archives, 23, 43, 65
Image copyright Mihai Simonia, 2009. Used under license from Shutterstock.com, 88
The Library of Congress, 30, 54-55

About the Author

In addition to his acclaimed volumes on the ancient world, historian Don Nardo has written and edited many books for young adults about modern European and American history, including *The Age of Colonialism, The French Revolution, The Atlantic Slave Trade, The Declaration of Independence, The Great Depression,* and *World War II in the Pacific.* Mr. Nardo also writes screenplays and teleplays and composes music. He lives with his wife, Christine, in Massachusetts.